Understand Your Border Collie

Understand Your Border Collie

A Breed-Specific Training Approach for Perfect Pet Behaviour

Sarah Hedderly

First published in Great Britain in 2025
by Authors & Co.
www.authorsandco.pub

Copyright © Sarah Hedderly 2025

Sarah Hedderly asserts the moral right to be identified as the author of this work in accordance with the Copyright, Designs and Patents Act 1988.

ISBN 978-1-917623-12-4 (paperback)
ISBN 978-1-917623-13-1 (hardback)

All rights reserved. No part of this book may be reproduced or transmitted in any form or by any means, electronic or mechanical, including photocopying, recording, or by any information storage and retrieval system without the written permission of the author, except where permitted by law or for the use of brief quotations in a book review.

Disclaimer

This book contains general information about training your animal. The information contained in this book is not advice, and should not be treated as such, and any training undertaken following reading this book is at the owner's risk. The information contained in this book is based on the personal and professional experiences of the author. Always consult your vet.

Contents

Introduction   ix

1. What the Border Collie Was Bred for and the Effects on Them in a Pet Home   1
2. Square Peg, Round Hole: Why Border Collies Are Misunderstood   9
3. The Unique Attributes of the Border Collie   19
4. Border Collie Body Language: How to Read Your Border Collie and Communicate More Effectively   27
5. Common Training Mistakes and How to Set Your Border Collie Up for Success   36
6. When the Wheels Fall Off: Mindset Help for Border Collie Owners   52
7. Your Border Collie Is Not Broken: Common Training Issues and Unwanted Behaviours   61
8. How the Environment Trains Your Border Collie When You Don't   76
9. Teach Your Border Collie How to Learn: It's Never Too Late   84

10.	Finding the Off Switch for a Harmonious Household	97
11.	Impulse Control for Your Border Collie: Build a Stronger Bond	105
12.	The Nervous Border Collie: How to Build Confidence and Trust	112
13.	Working With Your Border Collie	122
	About the Author	131

To Springading Batt,

One Friday night, I had no idea how impactful my Facebook scroll would be. The face of the most gorgeous black tricolour Border Collie looked up at me from the screen. I felt an instant connection to the five-month-old pup. I had been considering getting another Border Collie for a while, and my preference had always been towards black tricolour. I was open to a dog of any age up to a year old, but had not seen any that really grabbed my heart, until now.

Excitement and nervous trepidation ran through me. This could be 'the one'. I sent Battersea Dogs Home an enquiry and discovered he was struggling in the kennel environment, as many young working dogs do. Keeping an open mind since he might not have been a good fit, I arranged to visit him the next day. As soon as I met him, I knew he was coming home with me.

He was everything I wanted in a dog, extremely bright, energetic and keen to engage with me. He was called Hunter, but I wanted him to have a new name for his new start. My eldest dog was a spaniel called Spring, whose competition name was Spring Ading. From her name, I came up with Springading Batt for this lovely rescue dog, Ding or DingBatt for short. I chose the 'Batt' part of his name in acknowledgement of Battersea Dogs Home for allowing me to have him.

DingBatt lived up to his name. He was an extremely intelligent lad who played the part of a goofy fool. Some of his behaviour was idiotic, but he was far from an idiot. He was the brightest dog I had ever had the pleasure of living with. But with this brilliance came challenges. He had already learned a whole host of unwanted behaviours that took a great deal of work to unravel. He tested my resilience and, with no exaggeration, helped me become the person I am today. We often learn much more from challenges and failure than we do from wins and success. We also end up building deeper bonds with our more challenging dogs.

Today, Ding inspires many of the members in my online membership The Border Collie Academy. He is a living, breathing example of how DingBatts can be turned into Dreamboats.

Thank you, Ding, for being you and allowing me to be part of your life.

Introduction

While some Border Collies appear to come ready trained, this is not often the reality. These dogs are more unicorn than real life. To train your dog, you need not only time but an understanding of what a Border Collie is bred for and how that affects everyday life with one. Most people try to train them with generic dog training as if they are 'just a dog'. Many Border Collies are expelled from puppy classes for being too disruptive; by the time they hit adolescence, they are being rehomed.

Many Border Collie owners seek help from trainers without breed-specific knowledge, which can cause stress for both dog and owner. This leads to further problems instead of solutions, as is made obvious by the proliferation of Border Collies in rescue centres. One rescue contacted me for help as *all* the dogs waiting to be surrendered to them (after the rush to get a dog during Covid) were Border Collies. More than three-quarters of another big rescue's dogs were Border Collies.

You probably brought a Border Collie into your home to have a loyal companion you can share long walks and cuddles on the sofa with. They are intelligent dogs so must be easy to train, right?

No one prepared you for the amount of training they need to be happy and satisfied in an urban environment. Somewhere along the way, life with your Border Collie started to feel more like hard work than enjoyment. The reality of what it meant to bring a working breed dog into a pet home hit. You have started to dread those walks you thought you would enjoy together. Your dog constantly pulls on the lead, chases cars, and rounds up kids and cyclists... and if *only* they would come back when called. You get home and just want to sit quietly with a cuppa, but your Border Collie has other ideas. Don't even mention the struggle you have to hoover the house.

Instead of your world expanding now you have your adventure buddy, your world has got smaller. You are limited to visiting places where you can safely walk your dog and you can only invite certain people into your home, which makes you feel more alone. You know you have a good dog, but wish others had the opportunity to see their soft side too.

Owning a Border Collie doesn't have to be this way. Your house doesn't have to be in a state of permanent chaos, and training your Border Collie doesn't have to feel overwhelming. It is not inevitable.

When you learn about your Border Collie from a breed-specific viewpoint, you will realise you don't have a bad dog. Your dog is simply doing what they were bred to do. A Border Collie craves help and guidance, and when they receive it, they don't experience the drive to go self-employed and find their own jobs.

Border Collies love to work, have intense natures and are great problem solvers, which is why they are working dogs. They love clarity and structure around what is expected of them. If you can provide this, your relationship will grow. If you can't, they can find the world a stressful place because they think they have the big responsibility of controlling everything around them all the time. Some Border Collies happily rise to this challenge and find their own jobs that you may not appreciate them doing, while others become anxious.

If you feel overwhelmed or discouraged right now, it doesn't mean you are not cut out to own a Border Collie or that you are failing your dog. It simply means you need help in understanding your dog. The key to transforming your own DingBatt Border Collie into a Dreamboat comes from training in a breed-specific way that makes sense to you both.

That is why I created the Border Collie Academy and my DingBatt to Dreamboat Framework. It is a step-by-step system to help you navigate life with your Border Collie so you can help them become the best-trained dog in the park – because who doesn't want that?

The framework is a breed-specific training approach that has helped thousands of Border Collie owners improve their relationships with their dogs. Whether you are starting out with a puppy or taking on a rescue dog, this framework will help both you and your Border Collie thrive.

You will learn in this book:

- To understand your Border Collie – what they were bred for and why they do the things they do.
- Why Border Collies are misunderstood – how they differ from other breeds.

- Border Collie body language – what drives their behaviour and how to build a stronger relationship.
- Training essentials – how to build strong foundations.
- Common training mistakes – how to avoid common pitfalls and train for success.

I have helped thousands of Border Collie owners with various challenges of varying levels of difficulty to build confidence and clarity for both ends of the lead. Some needed help to find their Border Collie's off switch, others to teach a solid recall so the dog could be allowed more freedom, and many to make walks safer and less embarrassing by working through car chasing or reactivity issues.

As with many dog trainers, my work didn't start with other people's dogs; it started with my own. My granddad had Border Collies on his farm, and I remember his two black tris, Scott and Micky, from my childhood. My own first Border Collie was also a black tri, called Kim. Kim was a unicorn Border Collie who came everywhere with me and was a joy to live with and teach, even though I knew nothing about dog training. Pip joined Kim after a while, but it wasn't until years later my world was turned upside down by DingBatt, a whirlwind with many behavioural problems already established in his first five months of life.

It was no pleasure living with Ding. He bit first and thought later, had separation frustration, chased cars, chased dust in the light beams that came through the window... the list was long. But he was also the dog I wanted. He was loving, loyal and extremely intelligent. I had to learn about Border Collies to a deeper level and learn fast.

Introduction

We often get the dog we need instead of the dog we want. If we put in the work, we get out of it something much better than we initially dreamt was possible. Through tough times, Ding and I built understanding, and now the bond I have with him is the strongest I have ever had with any dog. My clients often experience this, too.

Imagine this: You are looking forward to taking your dog for a walk. At the door, they sit patiently while you get ready and clip their lead on. When you open the door, they wait until you release them through, then they orient straight back to you and wait while you close the door. They walk to the park on a loose lead by your side. Cars pass: they check in with you. No more ninja moves if a person or another dog comes towards you. At the park, you confidently unclip the lead so your dog can run with joy and explore the surroundings. You have total confidence that you can keep them safe with a great recall.

Energy expended and both of you satisfied, you walk home together for a relaxing evening in each other's company. Your dog is able to stay calm while you hoover and watch TV. You then do some mental training together as you both enjoy the learning process, and your heart fills with joy at the way you can work together. You can proudly show your dog off to your friends and leave them in awe of the training and what a good dog you have.

This isn't just wishful thinking. It is the reality you can achieve when you truly understand your Border Collie and work with them, which is what you can learn from this book. You don't have to find hours more every day to train, but it is about a way of life, working together. With a reactive and untrained dog, it can feel like your world has become smaller. With the right approach, your world – and your dog's – can expand and you can both feel more fulfilled.

These transformations aren't just possible; they're happening right now. Take Janey, for example: she took her Border Collie Cross to an enclosed field where he had a fine time chasing birds. She spent over an hour and a half trying to catch him by every method she could think of. Even when the next people who had hired the field arrived, she still couldn't catch him. When she finally got her dog home, she asked for help and support in our online community. She followed the plan and now enjoys safe off-lead walks and adventures with her best friend. She no longer feels embarrassed and instead is now proud of her dog's behaviour.

Similarly, Lisa's whirling, screaming, car-chasing Border Collie has been transformed into a dreamboat who she now enjoys walking and taking on adventures rather than feeling dread before the event and embarrassment after it.

Then there is Caroline, who has just managed to have friends over to her house for the first time in a long time. She has helped her Border Collie feel safe and secure by learning to read her body language so she can support her rather than put her under pressure. Long gone are the days of redirected bites, and their world is growing. Caroline feels happier and like life is returning to normal.

These stories aren't outliers. They and many similar stories are proof that you can train your dog for success. This same transformation is possible for you.

By the end of this book, you will understand what drives your Border Collie's behaviour so you can learn to work with rather than against them. You will learn why and how they are different from other dog breeds and why some general dog training tips don't always work (and can even make their behaviour worse). You will be more able to channel your dog's energy into a life you can both enjoy.

This will give you a better sense of connection with your dog: you can build a relationship on understanding and trust, and even a kind of telepathic communication where you know what the other is thinking and feeling. You can create a relationship where just being in each other's company is enough, and a feeling of love, companionship, trust and devotion that can only be achieved with man's best friend.

This isn't just about training your Border Collie for your benefit but meeting your dog's needs and helping them live a happy and satisfied life. All behaviour starts with an emotion. Understanding your dog's emotions and meeting their needs is the key to changing their behaviour, transforming your Border Collie from a DingBatt to a Dreamboat.

We will explore key areas that will make the biggest difference to how you work together. Here is what you will learn:

- What your Border Collie was bred for and how that can create challenges for life as a pet dog.
- Why Border Collies are misunderstood, as they aren't like all other dogs.
- How Border Collies use body language so you can communicate more clearly.
- Which common training mistakes to avoid so you can reach your goals.
- That your Border Collie is not broken; they are just a unique breed.

Each section is packed with practical advice, real-world examples and actionable steps to help you make lasting changes for you and your Border Collie.

Training progress is rarely linear and there will often be bumps in the road. However, by understanding what drives Border Collie behaviour, it becomes much easier to choose the correct training approaches and learn to work together.

You are not just reading a book. You are investing in your relationship with your Border Collie.

So let's do this. Turn the page and explore what drives your Border Collie and how they see the world.

Chapter One
What the Border Collie Was Bred for and the Effects on Them in a Pet Home

If you currently struggle with your Border Collie's behaviour or training, learning about this wonderful breed will show you that you don't have a bad dog but a Border Collie who isn't one hundred percent clear on what is expected from them.

In this chapter, we will look at the origins of the Border Collie and the unique combination of characteristics that make them such good working dogs, as well as how these characteristics affect their behaviour when they are kept as pets. This is not to say they can't make great pets, but they will likely need more understanding and training than non-working breeds.

You will probably recognise aspects of your own Border Collie in this chapter, which will help you understand them as an individual dog and therefore train them more effectively.

Your dog's behaviour is driven by the meeting of their genetics with the environment they are exposed to. Border Collies have been selectively bred for herding over many years; however, a Border Collie raised on a farm is likely to behave differently from a Border Collie raised as a pet in an urban environment. It is important to be aware of this combination of factors so we don't try to fit a square peg into a round hole when training these working dogs to keep as pets.

History of the Breed

Old Hemp (1893-1901) is considered the father of the Border Collie breed. He was a rough-coated, black tri colour, bred by Adam Tefler from his two sheepdogs in Northumberland, UK. Old Hemp was a quiet but intense, greatly admired working dog whose way of working, which he passed on to his progeny, became known as the Border Collie style. (More on that in Chapter Three.)

Old Hemp was one of the first dogs to be registered (posthumously) by the International Sheepdog Society (ISDS) when it was formed in 1906 because he had sired so many pups and had had such an influence on the breed. The ISDS set up their stud book about forty years later to keep a register of dogs all over the world who had been bred from known good working ability or trialling success.

The Kennel Club (KC) recognised the Border Collie breed in 1977. The KC's breed standard describes the breed's structure (appearance) and how that contributes to the dog's working style. They promote breeding to standardise the appearance of the Border Collie. Meanwhile, the ISDS criteria for registration are based on different priorities: they are more concerned with a dog's working style and ability. By breeding more for structure, it is possible that the Border Collie's herding ability will dilute. Research has found that 'show' lines – dogs bred for display at dog shows – are generally less impulsive than working lines. Despite this, a Border Collie should always have a working instinct, and it is their herding traits that sometimes make them misunderstood in pet homes. 'Bad' behaviour is often actually misplaced herding behaviour.

This fabulous breed originated from the borderlands between England and Scotland (hence 'Border' Collie) and was bred to work in a silent but controlled manner using 'eye' to control the livestock. To do this, the dog had to be able to work at a great distance from their handler, think independently, problem solve, react quickly and impulsively, stand their ground bravely, and have enough endurance and persistence to maintain their desire to work while remaining sensitive to pressure.

Border Collies' eyes are structured to detect movement at vast distances, and their sense of hearing is acute. This can make them prone to visual overstimulation and noise sensitivity in a busy urban environment. This sensitivity can make them challenging pets for first-time dog owners. A suitable analogy is that of trying to learn to drive in a highly tuned sports car rather than a basic family vehicle. The car would be too sensitive and powerful for the learner to handle. Many more accidents are likely to happen along the way.

While genetics has created a great working dog, the environment also influences whether they thrive. Our pet Border Collies live in dramatically different environments from those they were bred to live in, and this can create many issues for them. Let's consider the differences.

Working farm dogs	Pet dogs in an urban environment
Live in a kennel/outside	Live in a house
Lots of open space	Limited open space
Mostly off lead	On and off lead
Generally quiet environment	Noisy environment
Only meet the farm's own dogs	Meet many different dogs
Little traffic except farm traffic	Many cars and traffic
Visually peaceful environment	Stimulating environment
Lots of physical and mental work	Less intense physical and mental work
Herding	Pet, sport, search and rescue
Stay on their farm	Visit many environments
Not expected to be social	Wanted to be social
Independent thinkers	Need to be less independent

These differences will all have an impact on the dog's behaviour, although some dogs adapt more easily than others. Some individual dogs can adapt incredibly well, but this is not the case for all. For example, some dogs struggle with household noises from the TV or cooking utensils. Kennelled dogs are not exposed to all this noise and get quality rest in the evening instead. Also, the constant visual stimulation due to movement in the house and the wider environment can keep your urban Border Collie in a constant state of arousal. They then struggle to switch off and rest.

Not all Border Collies are social dogs; many would much prefer to work than to interact with people or other dogs while on a walk. Many chase cars and are frustrated by the restriction of the lead, so they pull hard or lunge and bark, which is much less enjoyable for the owner. Daycare can also be extremely stressful for some dogs due to the constant movement of others. They feel the need to control all that movement.

Do you recognise any of these traits in your dog? Do they run a greater distance from you on a walk than you would like? Do they like to make their own decisions? Are they overreactive to movement? Do they seem stubborn? Do they have endless energy? Do you feel outsmarted by your dog? A 'yes' in answer to any of these questions is a good thing. It means your Border Collie has the traits for which they were bred. Now you just have to learn the best way to train them so you can work together as a team.

The Herding Instinct

The Border Collie herding instinct is a truncated part of the predatory motor sequence. The predatory motor sequence consists of orient, eye, stalk, chase, grab bite, kill bite, dissect, consume. The herding part of this sequence should only consist of orient, eye, stalk, chase, and sometimes nip if needed.

Herding is instinctive and intrinsically rewarding to a Border Collie, which is why they will work all day for verbal praise and maybe a pat on the head. The satisfaction and feel-good factor of herding often means more to the dog than the extrinsic reward of a biscuit or treat. This is why trying to change inappropriate herding behaviour by giving the dog treats to sniff out often fails. The Border Collie's intrinsic motivation to herd is more powerful than the extrinsic reward they gain through sniffing for treats. It is also why some Border Collies default to controlling movement and inappropriate herding-type behaviour when stressed: it makes them feel better.

Border Collies like to work. If we don't tell them what we want them to do, they will go self-employed and make up their own 'work'. Outside, this may mean chasing anything that moves: cars, cyclists, joggers, even birds and aeroplanes. The restriction of the lead may make them frustrated when they can't choose their own path. Inside the house, they may want to control movement in doorways, attack the hoover or TV, and be constantly on the go with no off switch. Bored Border Collies can be destructive, chewing up furniture, scratching walls, and making toys out of anything left lying around. They can become overwhelmed in puppy and young dog classes if the classes are not set up to help them. The movement and stimulation of this environment can create a fraught puppy who is then classed as disruptive.

Some trainers think all dogs are the same and don't agree with breed-specific training, but there are others who don't like working with certain breeds. The Border Collie can be one of those breeds. When we examine what a breed is bred to do, it is easy to see why there are specific behaviours more commonly seen in some breeds than others.

I have heard various stories from Border Collie owners about experiences at dog training classes. When Linda's pup was young, she took him to a puppy trainer, who used to tell her off because he was 'doing that Collie thing again'. She said it made her feel inadequate and that she was failing her dog in some way.

Jeanette also took her puppy to puppy training. On the first day, one of the trainers said, 'Oh, a Border Collie, a farm dog; you will have difficulty training him.' Fiona was even told by a trainer that she needed to 'get the herding instinct out' of her dog!

These trainers might not have enjoyed working with Border Collies, but they were at least acknowledging they aren't the same as other breeds. Border Collies aren't for everyone. They can be an absolute joy for people who know what to look out for, and how to communicate clearly, create boundaries and teach an off switch. When an owner lacks understanding and precision in their training and is unable to teach the dog what he *should* be doing rather than what he *shouldn't*, both dog and owner can become really anxious. They can cause each other's feelings to spiral and become worse and worse.

Exercise One

In your accompanying workbook, you will find an exercise to help you identify herding behaviour in your pet Border Collie. It explains what you need to look for and how to assess your own dog, and encourages you to look for eyeing, stalking, chasing and nipping behaviour along with the target of that behaviour. This exercise will help you recognise the stages of herding behaviour so you can improve your understanding and prevent inappropriate herding.

Download the workbook here:

https://www.dingbattdogtraining.co.uk/workbook

Key Learning Points

- Border Collies originated from a dog called Old Hemp.
- The breed originated from the borderlands of England and Scotland.
- It is a working breed bred to herd livestock.
- The Border Collie is bred to be impulsive but also incredibly sensitive.
- The environment of a pet Border Collie is very different from where they were bred to live, which can be overstimulating for them.
- Herding is instinctive and intrinsically rewarding to the Border Collie.

Chapter Two
Square Peg, Round Hole: Why Border Collies Are Misunderstood

In this chapter, we will look at some common misunderstandings about Border Collies and debunk some myths. Not all the information about dog training on the internet is correct. Nor is it applicable to every dog or every breed of dog. Dogs cannot all be trained the same way. This chapter will help you understand why understanding your dog's breed and finding breed-specific training are important for you to navigate the available information.

We should always consider in dog training that an emotion comes before a behaviour, and a thought comes before an emotion. If you look for the reasons your dog behaves the way they do, you can avoid your training being scattergun. You can then teach the dog alternative behaviours that you would prefer them to offer. This helps prevent negative emotions arising through frustration and a lack of clarity.

While all breeds can experience the same emotions, some may be more prone to big feelings about specific things. Your working dog is bred to be naturally impulsive and can easily become frustrated if not given suitable outlets to meet their needs. Whilst I teach a lot about how the Border Collie is different from other breeds, there are also differences within the breed. For example, when working with car chasing Collies I categorise them into three groups: those that are scared of the traffic; those that used to be scared but now think it is fun as they have learnt the cars go away if they bark and lunge; and the hard wired herders who want to control everything that moves.

Some dogs are naturally easier to live and work with than others, and some I even think of as unicorns. These are the ones who are just calm and easy dogs who need less training than others to settle into pet life. The problems arise when this is expected of the breed as a whole. At the other end of the spectrum are what I refer to as the hard-wired herders. These dogs have a strong eye and an even stronger herding instinct. They are *all* Border Collie – the equivalent of a highly tuned racing car that needs an experienced driver for them to perform at their best. Then there is the range of dogs in the middle. These are Border Collies who show all the natural traits but aren't quite as strong or challenging as the hard-wired herders. They can still develop all the behaviours considered problematic, but are slightly more forgiving than their extreme counterparts.

In an ideal world, no one would expect to get a unicorn. If owners were aware of how much work they might have to put in to help their Border Collie become a well-adjusted pet, fewer dogs would end up rehomed or in a rescue. Many would have had their unwanted behaviour prevented in the first place. Sometimes the amount of work and training can feel overwhelming, but the effort will mean you end up with a great dog, and any fear that you will have to rehome your dog won't come true.

Debbie (one of my clients) has been lucky enough to have easy Border Collies... until she got her present companion. She says:

> Although Eve is my third (and most challenging) Border Collie, until I joined the Border Collie Academy, I didn't realise how very little I knew about Border Collies. Sarah has helped me understand how to read their body language and understand Collie behaviours and needs. I now feel equipped with the help and knowledge from the Academy to help Eve.

Prevention of unwanted behaviour is always better than waiting for problems to arise and then needing to find a cure. Let's look at how to avoid some common training misunderstandings that can lead to unwanted behaviour and a breakdown in your relationship with your dog. Here we will particularly demonstrate why training from a breed-specific viewpoint is so important.

Myth

All Border Collies should live on a farm.

Truth

Border Collies can struggle in urban environments, but can make great pets and sport dogs if you train them correctly.

While we must appreciate how hard it is for some Border Collies to live in urban environments, many thrive in sport and in active homes. When handled with knowledge and understanding, they can be incredibly versatile.

Myth

Dogs should be friendly and social.

Truth

Border Collies are not always bred to be social dogs.

Border Collies can find mixing with lots of other unknown dogs quite stressful. They were bred to live on farms where the only other dogs they needed to meet were those they lived with. This is why they don't always thrive in daycare or dog parks. They may want to control the movement of other dogs. Not all other dogs like Border Collies because they can feel intimidated by the Border Collie staring at them (eyeing) and trying to control their movement.

Myth

A growling dog is aggressive.

Truth

A dog may growl for many reasons, including during play.

Dogs have a ladder of aggression. They rarely want to get into a fight and will usually growl to warn that they are uncomfortable in a situation. A growl may be considered a warning, and we should always acknowledge it. If we ignore it, the dog may feel under more pressure and need to escalate their communication. Also, if the growl does not work and then they bite, they may start to miss out the growl and go straight to a bite.

When working with Border Collies, who are bred to be very sensitive to pressure, we should be aware of their body language and our own. While Border Collies herd silently, they can still growl as a warning in a pressured environment.

Myth

A tired dog is a good dog.

Truth

A *satisfied* dog is a good dog.

An over-tired dog's behaviour can be worse. Puppies often get the zoomies, steal things and nip much more when they are over-tired. Adult dogs can do the same, or become more grumpy or reactive due to lack of sleep. Also, if they are tired, they are less likely to be able to learn and will be triggered more quickly.

In the dog training world, many say that exercising a dog less can help their behaviour, but I rarely see a Border Collie with behavioural issues caused by over-exercising. It is much more common that they have not had enough mental stimulation or that the environment has been too busy and they are overstimulated. Border Collies need both physical exercise and mental training to be happy and satisfied dogs. They love to problem solve and use their brains. Mental training can be just as tiring for them as free running. This is why they excel at dog sports: if you are not interested in dog sports, trick training can be equally fun for you both. Rather than reduce your dog's exercise, you could take them to a quieter, less stimulating environment further out into the countryside.

Myth

Training a Border Collie is so easy that it is like cheating, because they are so intelligent.

Truth

Border Collies quickly learn both wanted and unwanted behaviour. Assuming that a Border Collie is easier to train than other dogs is why some owners get into trouble. While these dogs want to work and learn, if they are not given enough training or are exposed to inappropriate environments too soon for their level of training, lots of issues can arise in their behaviour, such as chasing cars or nipping joggers. Missing the first signs of problematic behaviour is a problem in itself, especially if the behaviour itself is reinforcing. Border Collies have many self-reinforcing traits that other dogs don't, for example, staring and constant movement.

Myth

All dog reactivity is fear-based.

Truth

A Border Collie can be reactive for many reasons.

They *may* be fearful, but they may be frustrated by being on a lead. They may react because they want to control something that is moving, commonly cars, joggers, cyclists, children or other dogs.

The body language is different: a fearful dog usually wants to move away from the trigger – perhaps another dog; a frustrated dog may react if they can't get to the other dog. This second emotion means the dog is more likely to react as a dog *passes* rather than as they approach, or they may redirect their reaction onto the handler.

Border Collies are often movement sensitive due to their instincts to herd and control movement, and their herding instinct is commonly misplaced onto things that are not livestock. A movement sensitive Border Collie usually stops reacting as soon as the trigger stands still. Trying to treat these dogs as if they are fearful rarely works: controlling the movement reinforces their behaviour, so the training needs a different approach.

Myth
My dog is stubborn.

Truth
They may lack understanding, motivation or trust, usually due to a lack of communication or a lack of understanding either on the part of the dog or the owner.

If your dog doesn't want to do as you ask, look at the reason why. Do they lack trust in what is going to happen to them? Do they have competing motivations, and what they are doing is more reinforcing than what you are offering? Herding and control are naturally intrinsically rewarding to the dog, so we need to create motivation for the dog to want to work with us instead.

Myth
Border Collies should be allowed to stare at other dogs as it's what Border Collies do.

Truth

Staring and eyeing are about control. That is intimidating to other dogs and is rude behaviour.

Many Border Collies become fixated inappropriately when they haven't been trained otherwise. It is important for owners to recognise the difference between the Collie looking around calmly and fixating on something. The latter can lead to the dog taking off to chase or reacting to something they shouldn't. If your Border Collie stares at other dogs, they are being threatening. As responsible owners who care about the welfare of dogs, we should be aware of the effect our dogs have on others, as well as the other way around.

Those are some of the most common myths about Border Collies. However, many owners also misunderstand their dog's impulsivity and frustration more generally. Border Collies are bred to be impulsive: they have to be able to react quickly when controlling the movement of livestock. A dog that has not learned to control their impulses can become really frustrated when put on a lead. This may appear as barking, lunging or biting, and the dog may become labelled as reactive or aggressive. Therefore, impulse control training is an integral part of the training we should be doing with them.

Border Collies love clarity. Some Border Collies appear reactive or aggressive when their owners have been unclear in their training, while others show their stress as anxiety due to the weight of the responsibility they feel. If the dog understands what they should be doing, or not doing, an anxious dog feels more self-confident, and a reactive dog is less frustrated and generally calmer. Both types need understanding and clarity from their handler so they know that they don't have to control the movement of everything they can see. If they want to access something, they need to know that the handler has the key, and they should look to them for guidance rather than acting first and thinking later.

Exercise Two

All behaviour has a function for your dog. The second exercise in your accompanying workbook helps you list all your dog's behaviours that you would like to change and then think about what drives the behaviour. It not only helps you focus on changes in behaviour that will improve your lives together, but understand how your dog feels so you can train with more empathy. You can work with your dog from a place of knowledge and select the most appropriate training techniques.

Not yet downloaded your workbook? Find it here:

https://www.dingbattdogtraining.co.uk/workbook

Key Learning Points

- There are many myths in dog training: don't believe everything you hear.
- What may apply to one breed may not apply to others. All dogs are not the same.
- Border Collies are not bred to be social.
- A *satisfied* dog is a good dog.
- Border Collies learn quickly both wanted behaviour and unwanted behaviour.
- Border Collies are movement sensitive due to their herding instincts and desire to control movement.

Chapter Three
The Unique Attributes of the Border Collie

This chapter looks at what makes the genius breed of the Border Collie different from other breeds. Their uniqueness isn't just down to their coat colours. You will discover why their unique attributes make them so good at what they were bred for and how the environment can affect them to such an extent.

We sometimes try to place our expectations of a pet dog on a working breed dog, rather like trying to fit a square peg into a round hole. Be open to looking at your Border Collie through a new lens and you will discover why some training that might work for other breeds doesn't work for your dog. If your dog is not perfectly behaved, that does not mean they are a bad dog; they are simply a Border Collie.

Behavioural Variation

Some research says that all dog breeds display the same behaviours; however, the study failed to include working dogs. Nor did it look at what drove the behaviours. And while most dogs can vocalise, bite, wag a tail or lip-lick, Scott and Fuller[1] found significant differences between breeds when they studied emotional responses to humans.

There is behavioural variation between all breeds of dog, whether they were bred to work or not. Bichon Frise were bred as lap dogs with a sociable and entertaining nature. Springer Spaniels were originally bred as hunting dogs to flush out birds from the undergrowth for hunters to shoot. They also retrieve birds and are known in pet homes for carrying items and parading them. Misunderstanding of this and taking away items can result in resource guarding issues. Border Collies were bred to control the movement of livestock, and a Border Collie who does not develop eye will not be able to herd, whereas livestock guardian breeds were bred to live amongst the livestock and protect them from predators. These last two types of dogs have radically different responses to livestock, even though they were both bred to help farmers.

Even within herding breeds, there is a wide variation in behaviour. For example, German Shepherds were bred to act as moving fences to keep their flock together on open land. They were also there to guard the flock. Every herding breed has been selectively bred for its specific behaviour pattern and can be further identified even within the category of herding dogs as a header, a heeler or a catching dog, depending on whether they bring the

---

[1] Scott JP & JL Fuller 1965 Genetics and the Social Behavior of the Dog. Univ of Chicago Press.

livestock to the shepherd (a header), drive the livestock away from the shepherd (a heeler) or stop the livestock by bringing it to the ground (a catcher).

Herding breeds strongly express the innate predatory motor patterns such as eyeing, stalking and chasing. Between the breeds, however, the grab bite has been differentially bred for. An Australian Cattle Dog is bred for a strong grab bite. The Corgi was also bred as a cattle dog, but the Border Collie should not have such a strong bite since it was bred to work usually with sheep. If a Border Collie comes from a line that has worked more cattle than sheep, they can be a stronger dog and more likely to bite. In contrast, livestock guardian breeds have a weaker predatory motor pattern and do not stalk and chase.

These dogs do not learn their behaviour patterns. They are instinctual and appear when the dog is in the appropriate environment and in the presence of the appropriate stimulus. A handler can only work with their dog's natural instinct to enhance and control it.

Skull Shape

Skull shape influences how our Border Collies see the world. Their slender muzzle and moderate-sized, wedge-shaped mesaticephalic skull shape make them much more efficient at detecting a flock than brachycephalic breeds with short noses.

Vision

The eyes of the Border Collie have rods and cones, just like ours. However, Border Collies have more rods and fewer cones. We have three types of cones, giving us trichromatic vision and allowing us to see red, green and blue; dogs have dichromatic vision and can only see blues and yellows. The rods are oriented in a more horizontal fashion than ours. This means they are much more sensitive to movement but see a lower spectrum of colours.

Not all breeds of dog have the same rod orientation, however. The eyes of the Border Collie are different from non-herding breeds in that their rods are *more* horizontal, making them *more* sensitive to movement. The way the Border Collie's eye is formed means they can detect movement at up to nine hundred metres away, which makes them very good at picking up movement when sent out to pick up the flock. This is why they can find all the movements of our urban world overstimulating.

Consider this when you tell your Border Collie to work at greater distances from moving triggers. It can be challenging to work on their reaction to movement. Work with your reactive Border Collie at distances they can stay calm enough to respond to you.

Eye

The Border Collie 'eye' is the intense stare they use to put pressure on the flock. The development of their eye is innate. You cannot create 'eye' in a dog that doesn't have it naturally, and it is difficult to work with a dog that has no eye. This does not mean, however, that if you have

The Unique Attributes of the Border Collie

a failed sheepdog, it will not develop 'eye' later and then inappropriately try to control other moving things.

A Border Collie's 'eye' usually develops at a young age, so be aware of it when introducing your puppy to the world. There is no known specific conditioning to produce this motor pattern, nor can you get rid of it once it has formed. Some say you should sit by a road with your dog to get them used to traffic; car chasing is a fairly common training issue to be worked with in this breed. However, if your pup already has a strong eye and a desire to control movement, you could, in fact, sensitise these dogs to traffic and make them *more* likely to want to chase it.

Some puppies show eye by eight weeks of age when they go to their new homes. In others, it may become more apparent towards adolescence. The ones that show it a little later may be categorised as failed sheepdogs early on, but still develop into good sheepdogs later. You should also note that just because a dog is rehomed as a failed sheepdog, that does not mean they won't display inappropriate and unwanted herding behaviour in a pet home. It may be that they were too strong with sheep or that they weren't brave around sheep but are comfortable displaying behaviour with people, cars or cyclists who don't respond to their behaviour the way a sheep might.

Eyeing behaviour can be intrinsically rewarding to the Border Collie. It is thought to be triggered by the anticipation of movement because they are generally unable to hold eye on something that never moves. If they want something to move so they can eye again, they may start to play bow or bark to encourage movement. You may have seen your pet Border Collie return a ball or toy to you, drop it on the floor, then run back so they can stare at it. If you don't move the ball after a certain length of time, they may bark or pounce on it or pick it up and throw it in the air to make it move.

Style

A Border Collie's 'style' refers to the way they work when herding. A dog could be either 'clapping' or 'upstanding'. Clapping means they crouch down flat with resistant sheep; an upstanding dog remains on their feet. Their style is another intrinsic trait. Similarly, a dog has an intrinsic amount of 'power', which can be difficult to define but is commonly understood as their ability to move the sheep. A dog with power often appears to have an air of confidence about them that livestock respond to. When a dog herds, their posture is called 'stalking'. This, also, is innate. It is found in trained and untrained Border Collies, but can be refined with training and experience.

Border Collies vary in their combinations of the above. Dogs that have excessive eye can lack power and appear weaker. They can be excessive clappers. This type of dog may be reluctant to get up but then rush in and grip a sheep when the sheep is too close. Domestically, they may lie down and refuse to move when a car, jogger or another dog approaches, but jump up and nip as they pass.

Dogs with great power tend to be upstanding and have moderate eye.

Uniqueness Amongst Herding Dogs

Border Collies are usually silent herders. Some research has found that dogs who bark more generally have less eye.

Huntaways, for example, are known for barking: they are generally better at driving than holding the livestock. Australian Shepherds also bark when herding and have less eye than Border Collies. Kelpies are the most similar all-round herders to Border Collies, but the Border Collie is the most all-round herder of all because of its unique combination of traits.

It has also been found that Border Collies generally have more dopamine in their basal ganglia than some other breeds, which helps them be optimistic and keep going in their work. They will repeat the same herding behaviour for long periods of time. This can also make training for sport easier than some other breeds and is why they excel at dog sports such as obedience and agility. While this is an asset in what they were originally bred for, our pet Border Collies can be affected if they do not have appropriate lifestyles and outlets. It can create a faulty off switch and the dog struggles to settle. Dopamine creates a need for movement. In turn, movement creates dopamine. This can become a vicious cycle, so they need to learn to switch off. These dogs may pace the house or even develop repetitive behaviour such as shadow chasing if their needs are not fully met.

Exercise Three

Herding is a truncated part of the predatory motor sequence. It is triggered by a reflex rather than conscious thought. You therefore need to discover what triggers the reflex in your dog and starts the inappropriate herding behaviour.

When working with inappropriate herding behaviour, you need to learn to observe your dog so you can cue them before the reflex neural pathways are triggered, until you have trained your dog and have them under control.

Think about your dog's 'eye, stalk, chase' behaviour. In what situations do you see it occurring?

List the triggers and behaviours your dog shows. For example, does your dog eye and stalk the cat or chase joggers, cars or the hoover? For a full example, visit your workbook.

If you have not already downloaded the workbook, you can do so via this link.

https://www.dingbattdogtraining.co.uk/workbook

Key Learning Points

- There is behavioural variation between breeds of dog.
- The Border Collie's eyes detect movement at up to nine hundred metres.
- Development of the Border Collie eye is innate; this cannot be trained.
- The way a Border Collie works is referred to as their style.
- A pet Border Collie that lies down and refuses to move is referred to as a clapper. They have a strong eye but are usually a little nervous.
- Border Collies are usually silent herders.

Chapter Four
Border Collie Body Language: How to Read Your Border Collie and Communicate More Effectively

Verbal communication has made us humans less conscious of body language. Dogs communicate their emotions with us and each other using body language. Reading your dog's will help you understand the emotions that drive their behaviour so you can communicate effectively with them.

By reading your dog's body language, you will understand how they feel, communicate with them more easily, and be able to support them when they need it, avoid putting unnecessary pressure on them and build a more fulfilling relationship. When you can differentiate between times your dog is scared and times they are herding inappropriately, you will also be able to train more effectively.

While you should learn to read the body language of any breed of dog, and some body language is consistent across all dogs, some is specific to the Border Collie. You need to understand both to communicate most effectively. Border Collie body language is often misinterpreted and this can lead to failed training because it is inappropriately applied. The most common error is the reading of herding body language (a lowered head and tail) as fearful body language.

To read your dog's body language, you do need to consider the whole picture to truly understand what is going on. To build that up, we will start by looking at individual components.

The first step is just to be more aware and get curious. Be open to looking at your dog in a new way. It will take time and practice to develop your eye and be able to read the subtle signals that your dog may show.

The Border Collie Eye

We have already talked about the Border Collie 'eye' – but can you recognise when your Border Collie may be eyeing compared with just looking around in general? Eyeing is usually a fixed stare, intensely focused on one thing. The dog may be still or slowly stalking forward. They may have tension in their body, and/or a lowered body and a low tail carriage. A stalking posture is often mistaken for fear.

'Whale eye' is usually a sign of nervousness, called this because the dog shows the white around their iris. The dog doesn't feel comfortable enough to move their head but wants to divert their eyes.

Blinking shows a softer eye and may be an appeasing gesture, as is turning to look away.

Herding Posture

In a herding posture, there is usually a certain amount of tension in the body as the dog's movement is very controlled. It is an undesirable trait for a working sheepdog to have a high tail carriage, as this usually means their state of arousal is too high, which can stress the sheep and lead them to make poor decisions.

The Tail

The tail carriage is very low while herding. Sometimes the end may curl up, and sometimes the tail may go under the body. This alone does not mean the dog is scared and wants to get away. If the dog is wagging their tail in a rhythmic, relaxed manner horizontal to their body, they are likely to be happy, but a stiff high wag can mean they are asserting a level of dominance. A low tail where just the end wags may show a level of uncertainty. A waggy tail is not always a happy tail.

Hair

Piloerection. When the hair along the dog's back stands up (piloerection), that is sometimes seen as a sign of aggression, since the dog seems to be making themselves appear bigger. However, it is more often the case that the dog lacks confidence and is trying to scare away his opponent or at least make them hesitate so they can get away. Piloerection is a sign of arousal, usually through surprise, just like when the hair stands up on your arms. In some dogs it stands up along the whole length of the back, while in others it may stand up behind the shoulders and over the lower back but not between.

Mouth

Lip licking. This is generally thought of as a nervous sign; however, be aware that dogs also sometimes lick their lips in anticipation.

A dog's lips can be drawn forwards or backwards. Lips drawn forwards in a snarl shows self-confidence, which may be mirrored by the ears also coming forwards. A snarl with the lips drawn back, however, usually shows submission. Snarls of either form are a type of aggression. Various appeasement behaviours can also show the lips being pulled backwards.

If a dog shows their teeth, this is generally a warning of aggression. Submissive dogs usually keep their teeth hidden.

Ears

The ears can be very mobile. Ears pricked up and forward usually show that a dog is interested in something they are looking at. The ears may be relaxed slightly to the side. One ear twitching to the side may show they are aware of something in that direction and are listening for it. Ears that are pinned back, however, show a dog that is neither happy nor confident.

Now that you have an understanding of the individual parts of the dog, look at the dog as a whole. A single feature may not accurately indicate how the dog is feeling.

Context of Body Language

You also need to consider the whole story. Take into account what happens before, during and after an event to work out what is going on rather than making assumptions from the behaviour of a moment.

If a dog is put in a situation where they don't feel comfortable and they go into arousal, their body might respond in one of the Fs: fight, flight, freeze and fawn are ways a dog may indicate they can't cope in an environment. My Border Collies are all different. Beau would take flight, Ding would stay and fight, and Sparkles would likely fawn.

The direction a dog moves can also help us work out how they feel. If your dog reacts to another dog, look at whether they move forward or away. Moving towards is usually more threatening or shows the dog has more confidence. Moving away shows a desire to escape. These dogs may lunge forward but follow it quickly with a jump back: they just want to keep distance from the other dog.

Rolling over can be a sign of submission in a nervous dog. Many people confuse this with their dog wanting a belly rub, whereas they would likely prefer to be ignored. A dog usually shows their belly to prove they are not a threat rather than to encourage engagement.

You should always pay attention to your dog's body language, because it is rare for a dog to give no warning before acting. If their previous efforts have been ignored, however, they will miss out parts of their repertoire and escalate their actions. Therefore, it is helpful to learn to observe the more subtle signs in their body language. If you have a reactive Border Collie, observe them closely as you walk with them. You may see their ears orient differently or they may become more tense in their posture. Their head may lower and they may eye, hardening their gaze. If you ignore these changes, the dog may escalate their behaviour by growling, barking or lunging. If you recognise these subtle changes, you can connect with your dog before they go over the threshold. You can help them so they no longer feel the need to react.

Another example of body language to look out for is your dog's freeze when they are resource guarding. If they feel under pressure when you approach, they will often go rigid. You may first see a change in the orientation of the ears, followed by a stiffening of the body, and possibly some whale eye as they try to look at you out of the corner of their eye without turning their head away from the item of interest. If you ignore all these signals, the dog may need to escalate to a growl, air snap or even a bite. Instead, you can stop your approach when you notice your dog's early signs of feeling pressured. Either cue the dog to move to a set area, if you have taught this, or leave them alone.

Reading body language takes time and practice, but you can start by being observant and inquisitive.

Your Human Body Language

Your own body language can also affect your dog. Border Collies are bred to be sensitive to pressure so many don't like being stared at or approached head-on. If a ewe did this to them, they would likely stand their ground and potentially nip if their stare did not control the movement. Turning your body slightly at an angle and blinking or sighing can help diffuse pressure. Also, think about the level of your eyes. A small child around the same height as the dog will be looking more directly at the dog, which will create pressure. The same applies if you are sitting or crouching down. If possible, allow the dog to come to you rather than you approaching the dog.

Teaching the dog to be comfortable around hands can be beneficial, as people naturally reach out to touch dogs without thinking how the dog feels. You can do this by teaching the dog to touch a hand with their nose. Moving body parts such as hands and feet can be targets for Border Collies to nip if they are unsure, feel threatened or want to stop the movement.

Our dogs can feel uncomfortable with other human body language, too, such as leaning over them or hugging them. Hugging is not something that dogs do to each other; many Border Collies react if human family members hug each other, as they don't understand the context of the body language. Teaching the dog to be able to stay calm in situations that are unusual to them is really useful here.

Some Border Collies struggle to be around small children due to their quick movements and high-pitched voices, as well as their eye line being nearer to their own. Teaching children to stand really still and pretend to be a tree can help diffuse a Border Collie that is trying to round up the children. Once something is still, it is of less interest to the dog. Learning about Border Collie body language and pressure helped change Caroline's relationship with her Border Collie. She says:

> *When we joined the Border Collie Academy, we were concerned about what we saw as Cara's increasingly aggressive outbursts towards me and my husband. We were at our wits' end and didn't know how to help her. We had been told by a trainer we needed to be more aloof with Cara and correct her by making a bark noise... also to walk her down and show dominance by walking at her. Not surprisingly, this did not work.*
>
> *In the Academy, we were taught about Border Collies' innate drive to control movement and how to work with Cara to lower the pressure rather than increase it. It totally transformed our relationship. I now understand the world from the perspective of an adolescent Border Collie, so I can work with her from a place of compassion rather than frustration.*

Exercise Four

It is now your turn to apply your learning to your own Border Collie. What does your Border Collie's body language look like in the varying scenarios offered in your workbook?

Under each heading, write down what they look like when you observe them. What are their eyes, ears, lips, tail and overall body doing? Spend five minutes each day observing your dog in these different contexts to truly understand them.

Check out the workbook for examples. If you have not already downloaded it, you can access it here:

https://www.dingbattdogtraining.co.uk/workbook

Key Learning Points

- By learning to read body language, you can understand what drives your Border Collie's behaviour in order to use appropriate training techniques to create success.
- Border Collie body language is often misread as the dog being fearful.
- The Border Collie tail should be low when herding. If the tail is held high, it usually shows higher arousal.
- A waggy tail is not always a happy tail.
- Border Collies are bred to be sensitive to pressure. You need to interact with them so as not to create unnecessary pressure and make them feel uncomfortable.

Chapter Five

Common Training Mistakes and How to Set Your Border Collie Up for Success

It is a myth that all Border Collies are naturally obedient and come pre-trained. Even this genius breed needs help and guidance on how to become a great pet dog. Some need more guidance than others. Usually, the brighter they are, the more trouble they find themselves in because they learn unwanted behaviour just as quickly as the behaviour you want, if you don't know how to prevent it.

It is always preferable to prevent unwanted behaviour from building than to wait until a problem occurs. By seeing the big picture, you can prevent problems from the start. Border Collies are particularly sensitive to what they are exposed to in the environment due to their movement sensitive eyes and their ears being so finely tuned to noise. Your

Border Collie can be affected by some common mistakes. You can prevent issues occurring when you understand how these mistakes can lead to unwanted behaviour. It is much better to control the environment so your puppy or dog doesn't develop common issues such as car chasing or shadow chasing than to have to work through them later on. What can look funny as puppy behaviour may not be so amusing later in life when they have practised and honed their skill until it becomes so problematic that it negatively affects your life and theirs.

Mistake Number One:
Not Training the Border Collie

The first mistake is not to train your Border Collie. As a working dog, they love to work and do something. If you don't teach them what you want them to do, they will happily go self-employed and find their own job, whether you like it or not! If they don't know that they don't have to control every moving thing in the world, they will take it upon themselves to try to control cars, cyclists, joggers, or even your family from moving around the house. A bored Border Collie is often destructive. A Border Collie that has used their brain is a lot more satisfied than one that hasn't. They may need more physical exercise than some breeds, certainly, but they also need mental training to be truly fulfilled.

Success Tip

Training doesn't have to take hours each day. Short training sessions of five or ten minutes can help satisfy a busy Border Collie brain. If you feel overwhelmed at one more task to fit into your already busy day, start small and make a training habit of just two minutes while you boil the kettle. As this becomes easier and more fun to achieve, add on an extra minute. Remember, Rome wasn't built in a day.

Mistake Number Two:
Ignoring What Drives the Behaviour

I often see advice posted on social media that a person with a car-chasing dog should go and sit by a road and feed the dog every time a car goes past. The problem with this advice is that it is generalised. Some will argue, 'It worked for my dog,' and expect it to work for all dogs. You first need to find out why your Border Collie reacts to the traffic. While some Border Collies may be genuinely scared and need counter conditioning and desensitisation, many others are displaying misplaced herding behaviour. Border Collies find herding intrinsically rewarding, so sitting by a road and allowing them to watch the traffic while giving them treats may actually sensitise the Border Collie to traffic and make them worse. When you take into account the need or emotion that drives the behaviour, you can select the best training approach for success.

Success Tip

Before trying to address a training issue, work out what your dog wants from the behaviour. Are they inappropriately herding, fearful, attention seeking...? Use the knowledge you have gained from the previous chapter for this.

Mistake Number Three:
Failing to Consider What the Dog Finds Rewarding

Inappropriate rewards may occur in all types of training if the handler does not understand what the dog really wants. Movement and herding are intrinsically rewarding to Border Collies, so they may not want to take food or sniff as an alternative. Even if they take the food, eyeing, stalking and chasing may all be more rewarding. If the act of herding is the most rewarding thing to your dog at that particular moment, you won't change this with food alone. This is why you need to teach impulse control.

Success Tip

Write a list of everything your Border Collie loves and then rank the items in order of preference. Place everything on the list, even if you don't like it. Include yourself on the list too. Use your dog's favourite things to reward them for the behaviour you want.

Mistake Number Four:
Giving the Border Collie Too Much Choice

You can empower your dog by giving them choices, because this can give them agency; however, with the intelligent Border Collie you need to be sure that either choice is appropriate. Too many choices and no clear boundaries can again allow them to go self-employed. Border Collies love clarity and direction, and are often much less anxious if they know exactly what is expected from them. They take their work very seriously.

Not all Border Collies like to be handled or made a fuss of, whether in formal handling for veterinary care or grooming, or just being stroked. Giving them the choice to leave or for you to continue can be really helpful if your dog feels conflicted in these situations. Many people misread a dog approaching them as wanting fuss, whereas many dogs approach to check out the human. They just want to collect information. Some may just want to be nearby.

Academy member Scotty started to leave pauses and check that his dog wanted him to continue stroking him. He has found that through this, his dog has become a lot more affectionate. He says, 'Previously, he would grumble and walk off after a short fuss. Now I can't get rid of him!' I used this same technique with Ding, who was conflicted about touch. He wanted to be near me, but did not always want to be touched. I would do three strokes, then take my hand off him so he could either leave or ask me to continue. This helped him relax and enjoy contact more as he knew he could leave if he wanted.

It is the same principle as your dentist saying he will stop drilling your teeth if you put your hand up. It makes you feel a lot safer for him to continue if you know you can stop him if it hurts.

Taking this further for grooming or veterinary work, you can help your dog become a lot more comfortable in formal handling by teaching them a clear start and stop button behaviour. I often use a chin rest for this: the dog is allowing me to continue while his chin rests on a chair, but I stop if he lifts his chin. The control this gives the dog creates enough trust to allow them to be treated. They know they can communicate clearly if they are uncomfortable without having to escalate to a growl or bite.

Success Tip

Look at areas in your Border Collie's life where you could use choices to enhance their life. Also, identify areas where you should use more management to help them not make poor choices.

Mistake Number Five:
Constant Ball Throwing

I do not advocate constant and repetitive ball throwing for Border Collies. This sometimes upsets people but hear me out before you form an opinion. It is often thought that the Border Collie enjoys chasing balls, but they don't always enrich the dog's life and can in fact have negative consequences for your dog's behaviour. They can encourage the Border Collie to play stay away in the recall – they come so far and then stand and look at you. The Border Collie is usually more interested in the ball than the person. When they collect a flock, they bring them towards the shepherd but focus on the flock. When playing with a ball, they focus on the ball.

A better game for building a relationship is to play tuggy, because you are more involved in the game. Ball play is more of an independent party for one. Ball throwing can create a constant state of arousal: movement releases dopamine and then dopamine creates a need for movement, so for some dogs it can create a faulty off switch if it is not balanced with enough rest and an ability to self-regulate.

Dogs that constantly hold a ball in their mouths can feed their own anxiety or frustration with constant chomping rather than learning to relax and change to a healthier mindset. Some owners give their dogs a ball to hold as a pacifier, and while the dog may then not chase or do the other unwanted behaviour, it could be argued that they haven't changed their emotions, so they do not want to do it in the first place. This is a management tool rather than a change of the cause or emotion behind the behaviour.

Tennis balls can erode teeth, and constant chasing with quick stops and turns can affect a dog's joints so a lot of ball chasing is not good for their overall health and wellbeing either. On top of this, if they are constantly eyeing a ball in arousal, it can make them seek out even more opportunities for eyeing or lead them to react to inappropriate things, such as cars and dogs.

I am not saying you should never use a ball, but be careful and aware of how you use it and of the level of your dog's training. Hiding balls for search games or playing catch can be fun, but I don't usually introduce balls until I have my dog's recall or reactivity skills where I want them to be. By then, I have usually built so much value in other things that they are not a problem.

Success Tip

Teach your dog to play tug with you and teach skills within the game, such as a release cue, bringing the toy to hand, and impulse control around the toy. Do this instead of repeatedly throwing a ball. Alternatively, switch ball throwing with searching for a ball instead.

Mistake Number Six:
Failing to Work on Impulse Control

Border Collies are born to act on impulse rather than to stop and think about it first. This is important when working with livestock, because quick reflexes will help them control the flock. It is important to work on your dog's impulse control, however, to keep them safe and under control. This is a key part of their overall training, as impulsivity can lead to over-arousal, nipping and biting as well as high levels of frustration. Impulsivity is linked to hyperactivity: the dog may be unable to stay still, unable to concentrate, exhibit excessive barking and excessive physical movement such as pacing and being unable to wait their turn.

Success Tip

See the impulse control chapter later in this book to help you work with your Border Collie on this.

Mistake Number Seven:
Playing With Flashlights or Laser Pens

The problem of shadow chasing is seen within the Border Collie breed more than in some other breeds. It can be extremely stressful and frustrating for both the dog and owner, so preventing the problem from developing is preferable to – and easier than – solving it once it has started.

There are many reasons why shadow chasing may occur. While health issues should always be ruled out, you should always take a holistic view in order to lower your dog's overall stress. With a Border Collie, you should particularly also check that their needs are met in both physical exercise and mental training. Bored or stressed Border Collies may self-reward or self-soothe by trying to control movement – including movements caused by light. Try to work out the cause by looking at all areas of the dog's life, from health and diet, the quality of their rest and sleep, meeting their needs and lowering overall stress in their life.

The problem with light sources, reflections and shadows is that their movement can't be controlled by the dog and this can increase frustration levels. Avoid using laser pens and torches at all costs. Just one session of getting your Border Collie to chase it may develop into a shadow chasing issue.

Shadows are present everywhere, and sadly, some people live with their curtains closed, trying to deal with the issue once it has developed. If a puppy shows intense interest in controlling something like this it can look funny, but the reality of a dog developing a shadow chasing issue can have huge consequences for their own and their owners' quality of life. Redirect any attention like this immediately onto something else, whether that be a toy to play with or for them to settle down on their bed.

Success Tip

Instead of laser pens or flashlights, try some trick training for mental stimulation.

Mistake Number Eight:
Thinking All Border Collies Need to Herd to Have Their Needs Met

Border Collies can be just as happy as long as they get a suitable amount of physical exercise and mental training.

Giving your dog herding outlets and playing herding-type games when they don't have basic training in place can make inappropriate herding behaviour worse. It can encourage more eyeing and make the dog more independent and impulsive. It can actually prevent improvements from reactivity training if your dog's reactivity is based on inappropriately wanting to control other dogs.

Herding games using balls are not the same as when the dog is working livestock because the ball does not respond to the dog like an animal with its own mind. Your Border Collie would probably pick it up really quickly and you might think it must be good for them, especially since some reactive dogs will continue to play while other dogs walk past. It may appear that it is helping the reactivity, but it is more likely that the dog doesn't know how to be when there is no herding ball present.

Sheree joined the Border Collie Academy with her dog, Ted, because he was reactive to other dogs and very impulsive. She was a good trainer and had put in a lot of work with Ted, but in trying to meet the Border Collie herding 'needs', she had been using lots of herding-type games. His reactivity was sky high and she was not making any progress with this. We went back to basics with his training and also removed the herding games, and she started to see a difference and reduction in his reactivity.

Karen had a young Border Collie that she had taken on as a rehome. At ten months old, she had already had three previous owners and had developed many unwanted behaviours that were common in the Border Collie. Unfortunately, in trying to find a shortcut to help with her car chasing desire, the previous owner had kicked leaves for her to chase and to distract her. This created an unhealthy obsession with the new owner's feet and also a worrying habit of grabbing anything from the floor if it moved. Walking across gravel or wood chip was a serious issue as she was frantic to grab at it and she ingested some stones in the early days, despite her new owner working really hard to manage and work through this behaviour. This in turn created stomach discomfort and other behaviours due to the pain and stress. There were also vet visits and expenses which could have been avoided.

Success Tip

Border Collies love clarity. Teach them what you want them to do rather than focusing on stopping them from doing something. Teaching alternative but incompatible behaviours will give them clarity and is much easier when solving training problems.

Mistake Number Nine:
Not Recognising the Difference Between Over-Stimulation and Over-Exercise

I often hear opinions about dogs being over-exercised as a cause of behavioural issues but I rarely find this to be the case with Border Collies. It is more likely the Border Collie is being exposed to environments that are too stimulating for their level of training. The dog is stressed by all the visual and auditory stimuli going on around them in the urban environment and think they have to control the world. This is a huge task that can be very stressful for your Border Collie, whose eyes are more sensitive to movement than your own, before we even consider their acute hearing and sensitive nose. Sometimes puppies appear quiet in these environments initially because they are overwhelmed and shut down. This is also more likely for a Border Collie whose eye has not yet developed so the desire to control movement is not yet as strong. Therefore, be aware of the effects of the environments you expose your puppies and young Border Collies to.

Success Tip
Before reducing your dog's exercise, think of ways to reduce the overstimulation of their senses. Can you walk them in quieter environments or hire a secure field instead, for example?

Mistake Number Ten:
Allowing Your Border Collie to Become Self-Employed.

Allow your Border Collie to become self-employed in your garden at your peril. If you allow them to chase cars along the fence line, taking them for walks will be more difficult. Some Border Collies will also chase birds or even aeroplanes in the sky if they are bored and have nothing else to do. This will again affect your recall out on walks, and a weaker recall will mean more restriction and less freedom for your Border Collie.

Border Collies usually love to be outside and many people struggle to call them back into the house. If your Border Collie loves to chase, teach chase games with you so to increase your value and they don't need to look elsewhere to meet this need. Use a long line in the garden as management and train the behaviour you want instead. This does take more work to start with, but through this you will be able to give them free time outside without them needing to go self-employed as their needs have already been met.

Success Tip

Never shy away from using management as part of the training process. In fact, I actively encourage you to use management while you build on your training. This will prevent the dog from learning unwanted behaviours and make your training more successful. Use leads and long lines, and do not give free access to areas where they are likely to chase inappropriately until you have taught them a solid recall and good focus on you. This will help your training progress more quickly.

Mistake Number Eleven:
Unrealistic Expectations

Today's expectations of dogs can be high. In times gone by, we were told to leave dogs alone when they were eating, and if they growled it was your own fault for going too near. This the advice changed to say we should be able to take their food away to show them we are the boss.

Some Border Collies are genetically prone to resource guarding if they feel a lack of resources. Some feel the need to fight for food in the litter, and others may have things taken away from them that they have 'stolen' in the home. Puppies investigate the world through their mouths and often pick up shoes or other available treasure. They don't understand the difference between what is and isn't a prized possession to their owner. If they pick up a shoe and get chased by the owner, they have been reinforced in thinking the item must be of value – but because they have had it taken away, they can start to stress about a lack of resources or the loss of items. Next time, they may fight harder to keep the item.

Success Tip
Remember, your dog is a sentient being. Teaching your puppy to swap should always be the preferred approach. Later, teaching them to bring things to your hand is a much more positive approach than chasing them.

Mistake Number Twelve:
A Lack of Enrichment

I always think that when we get a dog, we should aim to give them their best life. They have so little control over so many areas of life that we need to ensure they are enriched and happy. A lack of enrichment can make them bored, destructive and stressed. But enrichment is more than giving them a Kong. While some dogs love a Kong, others find them frustrating. Look at all areas of their life and ask yourself if their activities or environment currently make their lives better or worse.

Your dog's needs can be broken down into four main areas: physical, mental, social and emotional. Each individual dog will have different needs in each category. Experiment to find out what they really love and in what combination, but start by just being observant and curious. Look at the effect of the activity on your dog's behaviour. Even look at your walks to see whether they are enriching. A Border Collie that reacts to cars at the start of a walk but not at the end has usually had an enriching walk; one that reacts to cars on the way home but not on the way out has not had an enriching walk but has been exposed to something stressful.

Puzzle toys can be incredibly frustrating for some and highly enriching for others. A dog that disengages and isn't interested does not find them enriching. Some Border Collies like spending time with their humans. Ding was like this when he was younger. The more time he spent in my presence, the happier and more relaxed he was. If I had to go out for the day, he was much more stressed in the evening, even though he had another family member with him during the day.

You can enrich your dog's life by adding more sniffing time into their walk, walking with other people or dogs (if your dog is social), spending an extra ten minutes training each day, playing with your dog, setting up some searching exercises in which they need to use their nose or even just spending more time with them of an evening.

Success Tip

If you use enrichment to help modify your dog's behaviour, try to give the enrichment activity before any unwanted behaviour starts. Otherwise, the enrichment may reward the behaviour and create a behaviour chain. For example, if your dog barks at you in the evening even after they have had their walk and training, avoid giving them attention. Instead, *before* they start demanding attention, settle them down with a long-lasting chew or such like. If you wait until afterwards, they learn that their behaviour gets them something good and will do it more.

Exercise Five

To find out more about enrichment for your Border Collie, access a free presentation via this link:

https://pages.dingbattdogtraining.co.uk/enrichment/

Key Learning Points

- It is preferable to prevent unwanted behaviour than to let it occur and then have to work through it to reduce it.
- It is a mistake to get a Border Collie if you don't have time to train it.
- Do not use laser pens. They can create issues such as shadow chasing.
- Constant ball throwing is often not a healthy outlet for a Border Collie.
- Urban herding games are not appropriate for all Border Collies. They can cause an increase in misplaced herding behaviour.
- Try to balance your Border Collie's physical exercise and mental training with their social and emotional needs.

Chapter Six

When the Wheels Fall Off: Mindset Help for Border Collie Owners

Being a dog trainer isn't really about training dogs but teaching people how to work with their dogs. There are two emotional beings involved, and both ends of the lead need compassion, understanding and help to reach their goals. When we get a dog, we dream of a fun-loving companion we can share adventures, companionship and cuddles with. We don't often consider what it will take to help the dog reach Dreamboat status. Some dogs need more support getting there than others. If we don't get what we were expecting, it can be a harsh reality check and feel like the wheels have fallen off.

It's Not Just You

If your dog does not behave as you expected them to, it can really affect how you feel. Our dogs can mirror and bring up all our deepest fears and emotions. You might have feelings of frustration, guilt, failure, letting down the dog, feeling unloved, exhaustion, overwhelm, embarrassment and even anger. If at any stage you have encountered any of these emotions, please know you are not alone. All emotions are valid. It doesn't mean you are a failure, a bad person or that you have a bad dog. Here are some tips to help you reset and move forward if (or when) things get tough.

Be kind to yourself. We wouldn't speak to others in the way we often talk to ourselves in our heads. Be aware of the way you speak to yourself. Would you speak to others this way? What would you say to others in your position instead?

It is an interesting fact that emotions only last in the body for ninety seconds. Beyond this time frame, it is more likely that we are being influenced by the stories we tell ourselves about the situation. As an example, many people with a reactive dog may go for a walk during which their dog reacts to another dog. The reaction may only last thirty seconds, but it clouds their whole view of the walk. They keep thinking about how bad and totally embarrassing it was, and how the other dog's owner is now obviously thinking badly of them. They forget the fact that the dog had done beautiful loose lead walking to the park, past several other dogs, people and cars because of this one small moment in time. It may have lasted for one percent of the walk and was just a step too far for the dog to manage at that moment in time.

Try not to allow one minute of unwanted behaviour to overshadow fifty-nine minutes of good behaviour. Instead, learn from the event and then choose where to put your focus.

You *can* choose what to focus on. This takes practice as our brains are all naturally wired with a negative bias. It is this that keeps us safe from danger. Being aware of this bias and practising healthier ways to look at events can really help.

Because of the challenges I faced with Ding, I have a stronger bond with him than I had with some of my less challenging dogs. I had to dig deep into my mental approach to training when Ding came into my life. I decided to reframe the challenges we faced as opportunities to train and learn. I analysed any blips or challenges so that I could learn from the mistakes, prevent them happening again and also make a plan to train to improve the unwanted behaviour. We don't always get the dog we want, but we always get the dog we need. With time and understanding, the 'harder' dogs often become the best dogs.

You Can't Control Everything

Focus on what you can control, instead of what you can't. Does it fill you with dread when an off-lead dog runs towards you and the owner shouts, "Don't worry, he's friendly!"? I am often asked what owners can do about these dogs: the fact is you can't do a lot. If you put all your focus on others and their actions, it leads to a lot of misery and resentment. Focus on the things you can control, which may be where you walk, the time of day you walk or, most importantly, your relationship with your dog and their training. If you know that you have taken your dog into an environment that is too difficult for their stage of training, you can't change anything in that moment. Switch to management and remove your dog from the situation as quickly as you safely can. Sometimes you will find yourself in a scenario which doesn't benefit your training. Sometimes the unexpected happens. Nothing in life is perfect.

Dog training is a journey, not just an event. It takes time for both the owner and the dog to learn. If you only focus on the end goal and not the progress you make, you will be constantly disappointed and much more likely to give up. Look for small wins along the way and celebrate every step you take towards your goals, as this will help you stay motivated.

Progress in your training is never linear. It is natural to have bumps in the road. When you're in a dip, rather than feel defeated, reframe that failure as part of success in progress. As Michael Jordan said, "I've missed more than nine thousand shots in my career. I've lost almost three hundred games. Twenty-six times I've been trusted to take the game-winning shot and missed. I've failed over and over and over again in my life. And that is why I succeed."

You only fail if you give up.

As well as the voice in your own head, it is easy to fall into the trap of letting unsolicited advice or comments ruin your day. Maybe someone has made a derogatory comment about your dog on a walk. Maybe a family member has said something about your dog that upset you. Learning to deal with unsolicited advice is a skill. Ask yourself if the advice was valuable. Is the person an expert who could genuinely help you? Do they know you and your dog?

Advice we haven't asked for often only affects us if deep down we believe the same thing. Be honest with yourself – is the issue what they said or what you believe? If someone told you something you know to be untrue, it wouldn't affect you. For example, if someone said your Border Collie was a fat Labrador, you would likely laugh it off and move on. But if someone said something like, "You are making your dog behave like that,' you may take it more personally. They may say your dog is aggressive or that you should train them a different way. If you know that they are wrong, choose not to believe them.

Alongside unsolicited advice, don't guess what others are thinking, as you will never know. What you perceive as a dirty look may be because they are having a bad day, or maybe that is just the way they look. Even if they *are* thinking badly of you, they aren't likely to still think about you after the walk anyway. So why give them your headspace? In our membership, it is so lovely when others share how people have commented to them about how much their dog has improved over time. It just goes to show you aren't always being judged negatively by others, so don't try to guess what is going on in their head. You may be wrong.

Comparing ourselves to others can be disheartening. We can look at other dogs in the park and ask why our own dogs can't be like that. But we don't know if that dog was an easy dog from the start or if the owner has put in a lot of time and effort to reach that stage. Not all dogs that appear really well-behaved started out pre-programmed in ideal behaviour.

Focus on progress rather than perfection. Small steps all add up to big changes; big journeys start with a small step. The first step may be the most challenging to take, but it is the most important as it gets you started. Are you ready to take your first step today?

Sand or Stone?

There is a great saying that you should setting your goals in stone but write your plans in sand. Your plans may need adjusting along the way for you to reach the goal. Your dog may need you to break the training down into more steps than another dog, but that is ok if that is what they need and how they learn. When setting goals, always be realistic with time frames. Unrealistic expectations of yourself and your dog can kill your joy. We don't expect our children to have degree level learning by the time they go to senior school and we shouldn't expect the equivalent of our dogs.

You can learn beneficial techniques to help both you and your dog stay relaxed. If you feel embarrassed by your dog's behaviour and worry what someone may think or say, you can defuse the situation by saying a cheery, 'Hello,' and then turn back to your dog and say, 'Oh dear, that was dramatic,' or, 'There is no need to be scared.' Learning to control your breathing can also help as if you are calm and confident, you can pass this on to your dog as well. An interesting study has been done with people and horses where a handler led a horse along a track. Both the horse and handler wore heart rate monitors. First time, they simply walked along the track. The second time, the person leading the horse was told they would have to pass a person who would put up an umbrella as they passed. The umbrella was not in fact put up, but the handler's heart rate rose in anticipation and so did the horse's. This is an example of how we can subconsciously affect our horses and I strongly suspect the same is true for our dogs.

Through my horses, I learned how my breathing could affect my body. If I carried tension, my horses did too. But I found that I couldn't tense my body while I exhaled, so if I saw something I thought they may react to or spook at, I breathed out. This technique can also be used when working with your dog so you don't tighten your grip on the lead.

Box breathing is another technique that can help regulate your nervous system. It helps return breathing to a relaxed rhythm by breathing in, holding your breath, then breathing out and holding your breath for the same count, usually three or four.

Finally, if your dog is giving you a hard time, remember it is likely they are having a hard time themselves. The dog is demonstrating their level of stress, and when you understand this you can show them more empathy and therefore support and guide them in better ways. You are doing the best you can with the knowledge you have, and so is your dog. Don't struggle alone. You can choose to make a change.

Jane, a Border Collie Academy member, found that changing her mindset when out with her Border Collie really helped. She taught herself to remember that her Border Collie wasn't being naughty and that reacting to things was what he was bred to do. This helped keep her calm when they met any triggers on a walk.

Clare says, 'Lately, I have somehow managed to be calmer on walks, and he is doing better. I think I've adopted an attitude where I forgive myself if things go wrong and learn from it, rather than get frustrated and stressed out.'

If we do something regularly enough, we can make it a habit, whether it is a positive action or a negative one. The more negative self-talk we use, the more negative we become. We can do the same to help us move forward: creating positive habits will create change. Look for tiny ways to change your habits so they help you reach your goals. Find small steps that help you get started.

I have heard it said that the hardest weight to lift in the gym is the door you open to enter. Making that decision to open the door takes the most mental effort. Maybe your first effort is to make sure you always have dog treats available to use for your training.

Look at what is stopping you from getting started. If you forget to train your dog during the day and are then too exhausted at the end of the day, try to attach your training sessions to something you already do regularly. They don't need to be long to start to make progress. This may be a five-minute training session each time you boil the kettle or after a meal. While you may not notice the difference straight away, each tiny session will add up over time to big leaps forward towards your end goal. Your regular training habit will then show your dog good behaviour habits. The more they practise these habits, the stronger the behaviour will get.

Exercise Six

Our brains naturally have a negative bias. This is normal and keeps us safe from danger. But if we allow ourselves to focus only on the negatives, we can sometimes lose sight of all the positives.

List all the things you like and love about your dog. Check out the workbook for an example.

Access your workbook via this link:

https://www.dingbattdogtraining.co.uk/workbook

Key Learning Points

- Your dog can bring up all your deepest fears and emotions.
- Be kind to yourself and only talk to yourself as you would someone else.
- Emotions only last for ninety seconds. Be aware of building unhelpful stories you may be building around what could have happened but didn't.
- Reframe challenges as opportunities to train.
- Focus on what you can control rather than what you can't.
- In dog training, your progress will rarely be linear. It can be a bumpy road, so look at your overall progress instead of seeking perfection.

Chapter 7
Your Border Collie Is Not Broken: Common Training Issues and Unwanted Behaviours

One of the most rewarding things I hear from people who join my free online training challenges is that they now don't feel so alone. They realise their dog is not the only Border Collie to behave the way they do, and in fact, a lot of their behaviour now makes sense as they begin to understand why they behave this way. This lesson alone takes a lot of pressure off the owner who is just trying to do the best thing for their dog.

There are many unwanted behaviours commonly seen in pet Border Collies. This is not an exhaustive list, but gives a general idea of the most common training or behavioural challenges within this breed. By being aware of them, you can help prevent them from arising if you are starting with a young dog. I am not saying all Border Collies will demonstrate all these behaviours, but if you know about them you can prevent them from impacting the quality of life of your dog and yourself.

Most unwanted behaviour in pet Border Collies comes from what the Border Collie was bred for. Your dog is, therefore, not broken, just doing what instinct dictates. They need appropriate training to thrive as a pet dog.

Faulty Off Switch

Many Border Collies struggle to switch off and need to be taught how to do nothing. Teaching the dog to be comfortable relaxing is good for their mental as well as physical health. This topic is so important that it is covered in its own chapter later in the book. See Chapter Ten.

Car Chasing

Border Collies often react to wheels, including motorbikes, cycles, skateboards, wheelbarrows and wheelie bins.

Border Collies react to cars for different reasons. I tend to put car-chasing Collies into three main categories. Some Border Collies are genuinely fearful of vehicles, while some start off fearful and find that the car goes away when they lunge and bark. Their success means they now enjoy the behaviour and it becomes a game. The third category is the hard-wired herder who has always been focused on controlling movement and was never scared. This type of Collie turns their natural herding instinct into problematic, uncontrolled herding of inappropriate targets which are not livestock.

This category has their eye developed as a young pup and may even want to chase from the first day you bring them home. Car chasing is a safety issue for both the dog and the owner as some dogs even pull their owners over or into the road. Watch your dog for any intense interest in traffic right from the start. With this type of dog, work on focus and engagement with you first in less distracting environments before gradually building exposure to traffic into the training. Start at distances your dog can still respond to you and gradually reduce the distance from the cars. Impulse control training is also really important for these dogs, which you can read more about in Chapter Eleven.

Controlling Movement (especially in doorways)

Herding is all about controlling the movement of livestock, whether that be making the flock move or holding it still, so it shouldn't surprise us that Border Collies often have misplaced desires to control things if they are not taught any different. Doorways can cause pinch points in houses and it can be common for a dog to stand in a doorway to block others from coming in or going out. This can be directed at other dogs in the house or at people. The problems arise when the Border Collie feels they need to escalate their behaviour because they don't want their human to pass through. Some even resort to nipping or biting. If it happens when the owner leaves the house it can be confused with separation anxiety. While some dogs may have genuine separation anxiety, others are fine as soon as the person has shut the door. With these dogs, it is more about the frustration of not going with their owner – a case of FOMO.

Biting the Owner's Feet

Again, this is usually to do with controlling the owner's movement. It may look funny if a puppy jumps around in front of your feet. Some people then move their feet from side to side to encourage a game. The problem arises when the dog gets a little bigger. When jumping at the feet doesn't control them, the dog escalates to biting the feet.

Kimberley took her puppy to puppy classes and asked the trainer how to stop her puppy biting her feet when going up and down the stairs. She says the trainer, without warning, grabbed her puppy's ear and pinned her to the floor, saying, '*No!* ... That is what you do if she nips your feet.' From that day on, the previously sweet puppy went for anyone who came near. This was inappropriate of the trainer and can ruin the dog's trust and relationship with their owner.

If your Border Collie bites your feet, stand still until the dog disengages and then start to move again. Repeat until they lose interest. If it has gone beyond this stage, also teach the dog what you want them to do instead. An alternative could be following the hand. The biting of the feet can then be easily diffused without creating stress and conflict. Rather than just wanting the dog to stop doing something, teach them what they should do instead. This is a lot clearer for the dog and makes it easier for them to change their behaviour without stress.

Biting the Lead

This can be frustration behaviour with the restriction of being on the lead. It does not mean your dog is aggressive. In fact, I'd like you to reframe your thoughts about this. Your dog wants to interact with you. I usually solve this issue by teaching the dog to play tug. I teach rules within the game to give them impulse control and a good release cue. You can then use this to teach them to release the lead. Check out the toy swap exercise in the workbook for how to do this.

Lying Down and Refusing to Move

The most common reason for this with a Border Collie is that they have a strong eye but are slightly nervous. When something comes towards them, such as a dog or a car, their eye kicks in so they stare at it, but they are a little too nervous to approach to control the movement. They feel conflicted. This is referred to as a clapper within the Border Collie breed. This type of dog may then react as the dog or car passes when they feel a bit braver and want to move it away from behind.

Golden Retrievers are also known for lying down and refusing to move, and are often labelled as stubborn. Kate Bond from the Golden Academy, who works specifically with this breed, explained that these dogs often have pain involved when they display this behaviour. A similar behaviour seen in two breeds can be for a different reason.

This does not mean that a Border Collie is definitely not in pain. I have seen Border Collies with pain in the hind quarters refuse to get into vehicles as they didn't want to jump in. I have also seen them lie down because they need a rest due to pain, but the most common cause of the issue is that the dog is a clapper.

Dog Reactivity

Often, dogs who are seen as being reactive are said to be fearful. While this can be true for some Border Collies, they are just as likely to react out of instinct and wanting to control the movement of other dogs. Border Collies are bred to react quickly and independently while working. They don't wait for the shepherd to tell them to move quickly to the left or right to keep a sheep from escaping; they do it through instinct. A sheepdog would be taught that they can only herd and use that instinct when cued to do so by the shepherd. Clarity is therefore important. The dog needs to understand that unless he has been given permission to work, he should control these impulses and instincts. If the dog lacks clarity in his training, this can create what is seen as reactivity in the pet dog world. Being on a lead and being held back from what instinct tells them can cause barking, lunging or even redirection onto the owner. When they understand when it is appropriate for them to herd and when it isn't, their frustration can be avoided. Border Collies can also react to dogs coming towards them head-on and generally don't like to be stared at. They use staring and eye to control movement, so if something does this to them, they can feel pressured and escalate to a reaction.

Playing Stay Away in the Recall

It is common for the dog not to want the lead to be put back on at the end of a walk and to stay far enough away that they can't be reached, if they have not been trained to feel comfortable in closer proximity to their handler. Border Collies are bred to work independently and at a distance. They naturally collect the flock and bring it towards the shepherd, so when they do this they usually face each other across a gap. The gap between the Collie and the sheep and that between the dog and their handler is influenced by pressure. The dog uses pressure to control the sheep's movement but also feels pressure when being approached. When you understand how they both use and feel pressure, you can avoid inadvertently putting pressure on the dog by turning slightly to the side rather than approaching them head on. As well as this, consider teaching your dog proximity behaviours so they are happy to fully approach you.

Chasing Wildlife

While herding is a truncated part of the predatory motor sequence and Border Collies should not finish the sequence with the kill bite, dissect and consume part, it does not mean they have no predation in them. Many owners struggle with Border Collies chasing wildlife such as rabbits, squirrels or even birds. Some dogs may even kill or eat them if they catch them. While this is normal dog behaviour, we need to train our recall to a strong enough level that we can recall our dogs in any situation to keep them safe.

Each dog may have a different reason for chasing wildlife. While some may genuinely want to catch and kill the thing they are chasing, many will never catch their prey, so it could be the thrill of the chase they enjoy the most. Others may enjoy the eyeing part of the sequence and just love to stare. If chase is the most exciting thing to your dog, providing them with chase games with you can meet this need so they don't need to look elsewhere. You can train them so the sight of a rabbit becomes a cue to look at you and it means a chase game is available with you.

The problem with true predation is that it can be switched on with a reflex rather than conscious thought. Once the dog has gone past a certain point, it can be much more difficult to break the behaviour or recall the dog. You therefore need to learn to read their body language so you can cue the dog before they go into full flight chase mode. When you build your training with impulse control and recall, you can often call off the chase later but when you start the training, you will need to interrupt the behaviour before it starts.

Considering that dogs rarely catch wildlife such as rabbits or squirrels, it seems odd that they still want to chase. Failing to catch the prey can make a dog try harder next time. The thrill of the chase also releases dopamine with the anticipation of whether they will be rewarded or not. This in itself can become rewarding to the dog, just as some people become addicted to gambling despite losing their money. The anticipation of a reward is often more intrinsically rewarding than an actual reward itself.

Reacting to the Hoover

So many of my Border Collie Academy clients have to take their dog for a walk so their partner can hoover, otherwise the dog attacks the hoover. Brooms can have the same effect even though it is quiet. It is usually the movement that starts the interest, and then the sound on top can make it worse. Some Border Collies treat this as a game and just dance around in front of the hoover or broom. More commonly, they want to actually bite the hoover out of frustration at not being able to control this alien object.

If your Border Collie shows interest, don't allow this behaviour to progress. Otherwise, you may never be able to hoover safely again without putting in a lot more training. As well as the hoover, some Border Collies react to other household activities such as wiping the kitchen surfaces, opening certain cupboards, using food mixers, the dishwasher, hairdryers... There is usually both a sound and a movement component to these reactions and it is hard to determine if the primary issue is the movement or the sound, as they are associated. But when working through the training, I try to separate the sound and movement and work with each separately to begin with, before working with them together.

Reacting to the TV

Reacting to the TV is also not uncommon. Sometimes it escalates to many broken TV screens or owners being unable to watch the TV at all. This is potentially dangerous to everyone, including the dog, as well as limiting the owner's relaxation time. Again, the cause can be movement or sound, but the movement is usually the primary cause.

As described in an earlier chapter, our dogs' eyes are much more sensitive to movement and light than ours. A TV streams individual images rapidly one after another. Most TVs stream at sixty or 120 Hertz. As humans only have motion perception up to around fifty-five Hertz, we see a smooth stream of viewing. Dogs, however, see changes up to seventy-five Hertz so see a lot of flickering between images. Modern TVs are higher resolution and the pictures stream more quickly at a rate our dogs see more smoothly, so this likely changed some of our dogs' viewing habits!

You may notice a difference in your dog's interest in the TV if you switch to a new one. If their interest is primarily due to motion perception, they may react less when they see a clearer picture on a TV with a refresh rate of 120 Hertz. They may react to more specific things instead, like dogs or other animals, because they can see the picture more clearly. You may also notice that your dog sits closer to the TV than you. They do this because their vision is closer to 20/75 than 20/20 so isn't as clear or sharp.

Not Liking the Lead or Harness

Many Border Collies dislike the restriction of a harness around their body, even with extensive conditioning. Some also have big feelings about clipping the lead onto the collar. While this could be due to the restriction they feel about the lead, it can also be because of the negative associations they make of hands approaching them and a feeling of pressure. Teach your Border Collie to come to you to have the lead or harness put on instead of you approaching them. Play fun games around hands, such as teaching a nose touch to the hand, chin rest in the hand,

and a collar grab game where they target their neck to your hand.

Handling, Grooming and Vet Visits

Many Border Collies struggle with formal handling like vet visits and grooming. They tend to have bad reputations for nipping. Teaching voluntary handling protocols can be useful so the dog feels they can control the situation, which makes them feel safer. Use a start button behaviour so the dog can indicate if they need you to stop, which builds their confidence. This is just like at the dentist where you raise your hand if you want them to stop drilling. Because you know you can stop them at any time, you feel more confident in letting them continue. If you knew they wouldn't listen, but would just pin you into the chair, you would likely be a lot less trusting.

By teaching the dog a signal they can use to stop you or the vet from proceeding, they become a lot more trusting. Depending on what treatment is required, I often use a chin rest as the start button and lifting the chin off the chair or hand as an indication they want you to stop. While this protocol may not be suitable for every situation, it is often used with zoo animals for procedures such as blood draws and injections. It obviously needs to be taught before the day, in preparation.

Shadow Chasing

Shadow chasing can develop for different reasons and escalate to different intensities. It is a tough behavioural issue to work through, so should be prevented as much as possible. While some dogs may shadow chase due to health problems, it can also be a result of stress or boredom. It is sometimes also caused by laser pointers or flashlights. These shouldn't be used to encourage a Border Collie to chase. A one-time game that someone sees as a funny thing can lead to a long-lasting behavioural issue.

Barking

Border Collies are known for being silent herders. However, many owners struggle with them barking at other times, and it is a common issue that I am asked to help with. Constant barking can affect owners, other dogs in the family and neighbours and can be really triggering to live with. Consider the reason your dog is doing it, as they are unlikely to choose to bark all day long for no reason. While a few dogs do appear to like the sound of their own voices, it is more common for a dog to bark to express something in communication. They may bark to alert you that someone is outside the house or alarm bark when they have been shocked by something. They can bark through excitement or frustration, to gain attention, when they are over tired, to scare away something scary or to get things to move so they can eye or chase them.

Not all barking is equal, and learning to listen to what type of bark your dog is giving will help you choose the right protocol to help stop them barking. If my dogs bark in the night, I can tell the difference between there being some wildlife outside the window or if they genuinely need the toilet, as not all barking sounds the same. In the same way, I know which dog is barking as they also sound different.

If my dog needs to go out to the toilet, of course I want them to let me know. I also want them to tell me if there is a person or potential intruder outside my home, but I then show them that they can step down and be quiet and that I will take over dealing with the person. I thank them for letting me know and then send them to their bed so they can calm.

How you should approach it depends on why the dog is barking. Work on calm behaviour and impulse control with an over-excited dog . With a dog that is scared of things, work on building confidence and look at the distance between them and their triggers so they no longer feel they need to scare it away. If they are over tired, try to get your dog into a better sleep routine. For frustration, try to remove the frustrating scenario and work separately on frustration tolerance. If they want attention, make sure their needs are met. Also, consider that if a dog barks and we get cross and tell them to shut up, we are in fact rewarding them with our attention. Dogs are masters of doing what works.

Many owners try to solve barking by rewarding the dog for being quiet, but this can make it worse: the dog has to bark to then be quiet, and in effect, we are rewarding the whole behaviour chain, including the bark. Another technique that some use is to put the barking on cue so the dog barks when asked to and is also quiet when asked. Unless you teach this really thoroughly, you can risk the dog throwing in more barking as he tries to guess what you want from them.

I work to reduce barking by teaching calm and impulse control, and by not responding to the dog barking as part of a sequence. For example, you might get ready to leave the house for a walk or allow them out of the car while they are barking. If the dog thinks that barking gets you to release them from the car or through the door, they will do more of it.

It is important when working to reduce barking that you stay calm yourself. Move slower rather than faster, slow down your breathing and do not respond to the bark.

Some people choose to use anti-bark collars or devices, but I do not recommend this. They do not help the dog change the reason or emotion for why they were barking in the first place. It doesn't help them feel better or know what they should do instead.

Not all barking is equal. Learn to listen to what type of bark your dog is giving to help you choose the right protocol to stop them barking.

Reacting to Children

While Border Collies are sometimes seen as perfect family dogs, you need to consider that they do not all like being around children. Children can move quickly, have loud high-pitched voices, and this can cause stress if the Border Collie doesn't have a good off switch and doesn't know it is not appropriate to herd the children. For a harmonious household, it is important to teach clear boundaries for everyone, dog and children included. Make sure the Border Collie has a safe space where they can rest and not be constantly overstimulated with movement and play. Make sure the children have rules such as leaving the dog alone while he is eating or sleeping. If the children are not old enough to understand this, use management by keeping them separate with baby gates when you are not giving them your full attention.

Exercise Seven

Teach your dog to swap toys. Teaching a dog to play builds positive relationships. Through the game, you can teach impulse control, a release cue to help with lead biting, as well as how to swap items, which can help prevent resource guarding. For step-by-step instructions on how to teach this, visit your workbook.

Not downloaded the workbook yet? Here is the link:

https://www.dingbattdogtraining.co.uk/workbook

Key Learning Points

- Many owners feel they are the only person to have a dog with behaviour like theirs, when actually the behaviour is common amongst the breed.
- By being aware of common behavioural issues within the breed, you can help prevent them from arising in the first place.
- Most unwanted behaviour in pet Border Collies comes from what the Border Collie was bred for. Your dog is therefore not broken, just doing what instinct tells him.

Chapter Eight

How the Environment Trains Your Border Collie When You Don't

Learning doesn't just take place when you are actively training your Border Collie. If you don't train them, they will still learn from the environment around them, and this includes things you may not want them to learn.

How Dogs Learn

Classical conditioning is a form of learning where a neutral stimulus is paired with a natural response. An example of this is Pavlov's dogs, who associated a metronome with the arrival of food. The dogs salivated when they heard the bell before the food was delivered, as they had paired the sound with the arrival of food. The dogs learned this through association. Operant conditioning, on the other hand, is a form of learning through consequences. For example, if the dog offers a sit, we give them a biscuit. The dog is rewarded as a consequence of sitting, which increases the likelihood of them sitting again.

Dogs learn through both associations and consequences. Many alert bark when the doorbell rings as they have learned the association between the doorbell and someone being outside the house, unless we teach them that the doorbell is a cue for them to go to their bed. Some will associate you putting on your walking boots with going for a walk and get excited, but if you put on your work shoes, they know they are staying home and don't get excited. They may also associate certain areas on a walk with an event that previously happened there.

The environment we expose our dogs to can have varying effects. The environment may:

- Reward our dog
- Scare our dog
- Stress our dog
- Overwhelm our dog
- Enrich our dog's life
- Cause unhealthy interest
- Provide competing motivations
- Distract our dog from being able to listen to us.

Some breeds are more environmentally aware than others. Many people struggle with Border Collies due to their sensitivity to movement in the environment. Movement can trigger their desire to control. They may want to chase after inappropriate things such as cars, joggers and cyclists to control their movement.

The environment can be incredibly rewarding and enriching to our dogs. Big open fields where they can really run, water where they can splash or swim, plenty of smells of the local peemail, wildlife they can chase or soil or sand to dig are all natural environments your dog may like and find rewarding. However, if we give them too much freedom before their training is advanced enough, it may come back to bite us later on. Always remember that what is rewarded is repeated.

If we always allow our dogs to free run when we haven't taught a recall, the environment can become more rewarding than us and make recall training more difficult. If we expose our dogs to environments which are too stimulating before we have taught them the skills to focus on us, we may lose the ability to recall them and gain their attention when needed. Does your dog's recall fail because they are having too much fun doing something else to listen to you?

By teaching impulse control, you can help to include yourself in the picture. The Premack principle is of huge importance when working environmentally. This means teaching your dog to offer a lesser desired behaviour to gain access to what they want. If your dog has to offer eye contact with you or a certain behaviour when they see something they want access to, it increases your value to the dog as you are the gatekeeper to all things good. See Chapter Eleven on impulse control for further information on this.

When you first start working with your dog, you want to use management to control the environments that your dog is ready to be exposed to. Watch your dog's response to gauge the level of difficulty they are ready for to prevent problems from occurring. In Border Collies, this is of huge importance as eyeing can be intrinsically motivating. Be aware of the differences between the dog casually taking in the environment in a calm way or actively searching for movement and staring or fixating. Start small and gradually increase the level of difficulty.

Many Border Collies can go over threshold in the eyeing stage of the herding sequence and can no longer respond to their owner. If they can no longer respond to you as they are fixated on the environment, then the environment is too difficult for them at their level of training. Create more distance from the trigger they are staring at so they can respond to you again. Also check that you have really good responses from your dog in less distracting environments, and learn to read their more subtle body language so you can cue them to offer an alternative behaviour before they go over threshold.

Many people expose puppies to as many environments as possible in the belief it will make them more robust later on. This may be a mistake if owners confuse the principle of socialising their young dog with the principle of habituation. While the active socialisation period is around three to fourteen weeks of age, dogs will continue to socialise throughout their life. Socialisation is the introduction of puppies to other social species, while habituation is their exposure to stimuli or experiences that they may encounter later in life. It is important that the puppy is not flooded with too much stimulation. These puppies can be mistaken for being 'good' and calm when they may be totally overwhelmed and frozen to the spot. This may lead to stress and anxiety for the pup, and they may grow into a more fearful dog.

The other mistake is not to recognise when a Border Collie pup is inappropriately herding and trying to control the movement of certain stimuli. This can later lead to dogs who chase or try to herd inappropriately such as chasing cars or nipping children. As described in Chapter One, Border Collies often go self-employed and find their own jobs if they aren't clear on what they can and can't do. A Border Collie who is put in overstimulating environments may feel really anxious that they can't control all the movement if they haven't been taught an off switch and to be able to settle.

It is therefore a better approach to teach your puppy to focus on you first and then systematically introduce them to more challenging environments. Start them inside the house, then move to the garden or yard before gradually working in more stimulating environments.

It can be a challenge to work out if you should allow your Border Collie to look at the environment or not. You want them to feel safe and secure and be able to enjoy investigating the environment, but you do not want to allow them to fixate or learn to ignore you if they find the environment more rewarding. In general, I would allow a nervous dog more time to check out the environment so they can work out that they are safe. With an impulsive, hard-eyed dog, spend more time working on focus and engaging with you so they don't practise unwanted chasing behaviour until they have stronger recall training.

In adolescence, the Border Collie, just like all other species, will naturally become more impulsive, braver and want to investigate the environment further afield from the safety of their handler. Added to the fact that they are already bred to be impulsive, this means they will want to investigate the world even more. In contrast, puppies usually look more to their handlers for support, so it is not unusual to suddenly lose your dog's recall to the environment at this time. You may need to revert to more management around the exposure and freedom you give your dog at this time if they struggle to listen.

Whenever you teach a behaviour, first teach it at an easy level, in a non-distracting environment to create success. You can then take it to a low distraction environment and gradually increase the level of difficulty of the environment the dog can work with. To select the level of difficulty, think of the three Ds of distraction, distance and duration. The level of distraction may apply to the speed of something moving, the number of dogs or people in the environment or the sounds in the environment. Distance can relate to how far away from the trigger your dog is or how far away from you your dog is. Duration might be the length of time your dog is exposed to an environment or how long you want the dog to do something. Only increase the level of difficulty of one of the Ds at a time: if you are reducing the distance from cars, don't move to a busier road at the same time.

Dogs learn differently from humans and do not usually generalise their training (as people do) to new environments. They are contextual in their learning, so as well as learning the cue, they learn the context of the environment they were taught in. Therefore, if the environment is part of the cue, when you change the environment, the cue will not mean the same thing to the dog. You need to teach a behaviour in many environments before the dog can generalise it to all environments and situations. This can be extremely frustrating for us humans, who are great at generalising.

Be aware of the range and changes in the environment to fully understand what your dog does and doesn't know. Environments vary in types: open spaces, narrow vistas, visually busy, loud or quiet, various smells, water, other dogs, people, novelty and even the weather.

Dog parks or doggy day care, where there is constant movement that they can't control, can be totally overwhelming for many Border Collies. They often fail to be able to switch off and return home totally exhausted. This is not always a happy and satisfied dog, as some become so frustrated they become reactive to other dogs due to the constant need to control their movement. While many owners feel they are doing the right thing by not leaving their dog alone while they are at work or think their dog needs to spend time with other dogs, these environments can be really challenging from the Border Collie's perspective.

Border Collies can often struggle with pubs and cafes, too. They are usually smaller environments where the dog may feel trapped and where they don't have an escape route. People are moving around and approaching. Some people may want to interact with the dog without asking if the dog is ok with this first. Border Collies use staring to intimidate and control the movement of livestock, so it is understandable if they feel uncomfortable and under pressure if they are being stared at and approached head-on by a well-meaning person who doesn't understand how to read their body language.

Exercise Eight

Check out your workbook for an exercise in observation that will help you understand the effects of the environment on your dog. This will give you useful information about the environment levels where they can respond to you, what they like most and what they may not like, where they can succeed and where they can't. This will help inform your training.

https://www.dingbattdogtraining.co.uk/workbook

Key Learning Points

- Your dog is learning all the time, not just when you train them.
- Border Collies can be more sensitive to the environment than some other breeds due to their eyes being finely tuned to detect movement.
- The environment can be enriching and rewarding for your dog as well as overstimulating.
- Build up exposure to more challenging environments gradually in your training.
- Use the environment to reward your dog.
- Dogs are contextual learners and do not generalise their training easily to different environments.

Chapter Nine

Teach Your Border Collie How to Learn: It's Never Too Late

There are many foundations to consider at the start of your training or even before you start to train. Without strong foundations, you have nothing to build on. Just like a house with poor foundations, it will fall down without them.

The best time to train foundations is now, regardless of the age of your dog. If they are a puppy, it will help with their learning and life skills. If they are an older dog that you have had for a while, it is never too late to start. Older dogs can learn new tricks and dogs more advanced in their training can always benefit from strengthening their foundations to help maintain their great behaviour. The most important thing is to work at the speed of you and your dog. Training is not a race but rather a journey to enjoy throughout life.

Advanced training is the basics done really well. Top trainers spend more time on the basics than amateurs who often prefer to train what look to be more impressive skills. Never feel like you are failing by spending time working on foundation skills, as they will serve you well with your ongoing training, and you may fail to succeed without them.

Foundations can mean different things to different people, but here I want to take a look at what can prevent our Border Collies from being able to learn and progress with their training. Each dog is different so consider your own dog in relation to the different aspects in this chapter. Are there holes in their education that you need to fill for them to be able to progress?

You already know that our chosen genius working breed likes to be on the go. This can mean they struggle to settle and get the amount of rest they need to function optimally. Just like a tired toddler, a tired Border Collie can create chaos and make poor decisions. Dogs need lots more sleep than humans. Puppies may need between sixteen and twenty hours a day, while adult dogs may need a minimum of fourteen to sixteen hours. If you struggle with your dog's behaviour, it is worth keeping a diary to see how much rest and sleep they are getting. If you feel your dog does not sleep enough, try adding extra nap time in a quiet part of the house where there are no stimuli so they can learn to switch off.

Poor health or pain are other factors that will affect your Border Collie's ability to learn. You can't train away pain or even a poor diet. With any sudden change in behaviour, always start here rather than looking straight at training alone.

There are many labels used in the training world to describe the type of training we choose to use. I choose to use rewards and positive reinforcement, but this does not mean I don't also have clear boundaries for my Border Collies. This type of dog thrives on clarity. When they know what is wanted of them, they take their job very seriously. Just because we train with rewards doesn't mean there isn't fallout. If the training is grey and unclear, they can become frustrated, especially when rewards are withheld or our timing is poor, as it provides unclear communication. The better your foundation skills, the easier, kinder and less stressful it will be for the dog.

Your dog will always show you what they know with their behaviour. Often, what we think they know and what the dog does know are two different things. We can then blame the dog for being stubborn or stupid, but we could argue that the dog is seldom wrong. They are showing us what they understand and have the motivation to do. If your dog does not do as you ask, first look at yourself to see if your cues are clear and if you have a previous history in motivating them to want to complete the task.

Marker or Clicker Training

When training, I use a marker to tell the dog they have offered the correct behaviour and a reward is coming. Markers may be a word or verbal sound or a clicker. Some dogs are scared of the sound of a clicker. If this is the case, start with a pen that clicks as you push out the nib. The advantage of a clicker is that it always sounds the same, so it is consistent and clear for the dog; however, look at the effect of the click as it can be too arousing for some dogs. You can use a marker word instead, which should be a short sharp sound. 'Yip' is a commonly used marker word.

A marker is classed as a secondary reinforcer. It is a promise that a reward is available and as it becomes paired with the reward becomes valuable in itself. If I ask my dog to sit, I use my marker as his bottom touches the floor and then reward my dog. If my criteria are for my dog to sit for three seconds, I ask my dog to sit, count to three, use my marker and reward the dog.

To be effective, mark and deliver the reward as two separate actions. If your hand reaches for the food reward as you use the marker, the dog will likely focus on the moving hand, and this action will overshadow the marker and make the training less effective. Try to pause for a second between using the marker and moving to reward.

Rewards and Reinforcement

When you use rewards-based training, you need to know what your dog likes most and what is valuable to the dog to be able to reinforce a behaviour. When a behaviour has been reinforced, it is more likely to be repeated. Some dogs love to swim, others like to run, some want to approach a friend to play, while others want to sniff. You can use anything the dog likes and wants as a reward as long as it is safe and appropriate to do so. Food and toys are the two easiest things to use to reward your dog. Food can be used for calming and precision for static behaviours, and toys can be used when you want more excitement or drive.

I am frequently asked by clients what to do if their dogs won't take food or play. Here is the answer I give, as this is about building the foundations for rewards before you start to train the dog.

Food Rewards

As part of survival, dogs need to eat. If they won't take food, there is a reason for this. For some dogs, the answer is complex, but sometimes it is a relatively quick fix. The first thing to consider is the dog's gut health. Is the dog healthy? This may mean speaking to a vet and/or nutritionist. A food diary can help you relate what they are fed to their behaviour. In the most simplistic terms, does your dog like their food? Try different foods and see what your dog would select if given the choice. It may not be what you would consider high value, but if your dog likes it, go with it. Ding is mad for carrots: they are really high value for him. Sparkles is the same for a malted milk biscuit, which I would have expected to be a low value treat.

Next, look at how you feed your dog. Do not leave food down all the time for the dog to pick at. Offer two meals a day, and if they walk away from the food, don't leave it there. Instead, pick it up and only feed again at the next meal time. Healthy dogs will not starve themselves. Some free-fed dogs subtly use food as a resource to guard and feel stressed about it being there, so it can also help them relax if it is picked up. Be sure not to overfeed your dog. If they are full, they won't want to train for more food. If this is the case, reduce their portion size.

The environment can also affect whether your dog will take food. A dog that is scared, stressed or overwhelmed is less likely to eat. If this is the case, start in lower distraction environments. Go back to the place where they could take food and build again from there. With Border Collies, arousal can also mean they stop taking food as movement is innately rewarding to them. Some stop taking food on a walk as they just want to run or get somewhere. If this is the case, you may need to make the walk more boring so their arousal lowers. Once they have taken the food, move forward again. Border Collie Academy member Gayle's Border Collie wouldn't take food on walks. She slowed down and waited for him to take a piece of food before continuing on her walk. In just two days, he was happily taking food for the first time on walks.

My young Border Collie, Beau, refused to take food as a youngster. I noticed this early in two specific environments so I knew I had to change this to make training him easier later on. The first scenario was when I was teaching him to sit so I could put his food bowl down. He was so excited about the food bowl that he lacked impulse control and couldn't hold the sit. My plan was to take food from the bowl to help him maintain the sit as the bowl went down. The sight of the bowl was too much for him to be able to take a piece of food from my hand, even though it was the same food. The other scenario was at my courtyard gate. The prospect of going running in the fields was so exciting that he couldn't take food inside the gate.

Eating is a behaviour and so can be taught. I used the Premack principle in both of these cases and he hasn't refused food since. The Premack principle means the dog has to offer a lesser desired behaviour to get access to what he wants. You have probably come across this if your parents told you to eat your vegetables so you could have dessert when you were a child. Beau had to eat one tiny piece of food to be released either to his food bowl or through the gate.

Food delivery can also change the food value. Many Border Collies like catching food that is thrown in the air or chasing a piece of food that is bowled along the floor. Animating the food can make the food more interesting than just posting it into their mouths.

Food rewards are also not about bribing the dog. If we use food to bribe a dog into a situation where they are uncomfortable, we can lose their trust, poison their emotion around the food, and create conflict around the food. An example of this is giving food to a stranger to feed to your dog that isn't comfortable around people. The dog may want the food so they go to take it, but then may feel so uncomfortable being that close to the person that they snap as they aren't confident enough to move away.

Play

Playing with your dog should be fun for both parties. You can teach lots of impulse control exercises through play. Play after a training session has also been shown to help with memory around the training and learning. I am a fan of playing tuggy as this is an interactive game that can raise your value to the dog: it should be more fun for the dog while you hold the other end of the toy than for them to hold the toy by themselves. When playing, try to match the energy of your dog. If you have less enthusiasm than your dog, you may appear boring, whereas if you are too energetic for a shy dog, they may feel pressure and lose confidence in play. Playing tug with your dog will not make them aggressive. You should, however, have rules within the game and teach the dog how to play in a way you can both enjoy.

Border Collies are extremely sensitive to pressure so you could start to teach the game on longer handled chaser style toys so proximity is not so intense. As the dog starts to enjoy the game, you can move to a shorter handled toy. Teaching toy swap with two toys can help teach a dog to release the toy. Teaching a release is a really important part of your foundations. If you can't get the dog to release the toy, you can struggle to train several repetitions of a behaviour. It is also important to build on your dog's play skills before using play as a reward in training.

Teaching your dog to switch between food and toys is another useful skill that will ensure that arousal doesn't affect whether they can take food or not. Play for a short time, then switch to releasing the toy and taking some food, then switch back to play. In an ideal world, we would work towards our dogs liking food and toys equally. Each dog is likely to have a preference, but it makes training easier if we can teach this as a foundation skill as well.

Luring

Teaching your dog to follow a lure is really useful in being able to transport them from place to place as well as within sports and general training. You can start by teaching the dog to follow some food and then move it on to following your hand or a target stick. Following a lure may be useful if you need to move your Border Collie away from something or someone. Don't confuse this with bribing your dog into an environment they don't feel safe in, though, as this will lose you your dog's trust. To teach them to follow a lure, start with some food in your hand just in front of their nose. Move it away from your dog just an inch or two, and as the dog follows, use your marker and let the dog have the food. Gradually increase the distance you move your hand.

Shaping

Shaping is a great training technique for teaching dogs how to work things out rather than quitting or getting frustrated. Frustration occurs in life and so we can use shaping to help the dog become more resilient. A dog that reacts on a walk may escalate quickly to frustration if they have never been shown how to work things out. Interestingly, the human often gets frustrated while learning shaping too as their focus is often more on teaching the end behaviour rather than about teaching incremental steps. But learning in general is frustrating so learning how to problem solve and work things out can really build confidence in the learner.

Shaping is where the dog is marked and rewarded for each tiny incremental step towards an end behaviour. It is like a game of hotter/colder where you have to guess what the teacher wants you to do. Each time they say *hotter*, it means you have completed a step towards the end behaviour. Start with very simple exercises and increase the difficulty level as the dog understands what shaping is.

One of the first exercises I shape my new puppies or dogs to do is to put their front feet onto a block. I put the block down, and as soon as my dog shows any interest in the block, I mark and reward the dog. Each step towards the block will be marked and rewarded until their front two feet are on the block. I can then throw a reset treat and start again until the dog comes straight back and places his paws straight onto the block. If I want to name this behaviour, I could add a verbal cue as soon as they have eaten the reset treat. I may then shape my dog to stand in a box or go around an object.

Capturing

Capturing is where we reward the dog for behaviours the dog already does. Rewarding behaviours you like makes them stronger and more likely to be repeated. The downside of this as a training technique is that the dog needs to offer the behaviour already for you to be able to capture it. While capturing can be a useful skill, I don't often capture calm behaviours in my Border Collies. If the dog is settled down in their bed and I go and reward them, I find it often wakes them up and puts them into work mode, negating the goal I wanted to reach. I have used capturing to reward my dogs stretching in a play bow before, and also as a trick where Mini now sneezes on the cue, 'Have you got a cold?' I appreciate that it isn't part of a dog's essential training, though.

Targeting

The most common behaviour people teach as a target behaviour is 'Paw', but then wonder why the dog paws everyone. Nose touches, where the dog touches the person's hand with their nose, are great to build positive relationships around hands. This is also a good proximity behaviour to use in recall. Chin target, where the dog understands to place his chin on a hand or chair, is great for calm and voluntary handling behaviour. Foot targeting or mat work is good to be able to send a dog to an area. Any part of the dog's body could be used, and the items you choose to use as targets can also be many. Teaching paw targeting can help with body awareness and build confidence.

Focus

Border Collies love to stare at things. It is innately rewarding to them. We can and should use this natural skill to engage our Border Collies because if we don't, they will be more than happy to find other things in the environment to stare at, and this can be problematic. Find a balance in your training where you are the most important thing to them but they don't need to look to you all the time. They should still be allowed to be a dog, but you need to be able to interrupt any inappropriate staring at other dogs and prevent them from stalking and chasing joggers, cyclists or cars.

While Border Collies like to stare to control, they often feel pressured if stared at. Rewarding your dog for giving you eye contact can help their focus on you. If you have a dog who finds eye contact uncomfortable, start by holding a treat in front of your eyes, then mark and reward your dog for looking. Gradually increase the length of time they look before using your marker until they are happy to look without the treat in front of your eyes.

Proofing

Teaching the initial behaviour is the easy part of any training; proofing the behaviour so it works in any environment takes a lot longer. Dogs learn in a literal way and do not generalise as well as humans. Just because you have taught your Border Collie to sit inside the house doesn't mean they will be able to do it in the garden or park. Teach your Border Collie first in an easy environment and then gradually proof the behaviour until they can do it at any time, anywhere.

Consider the three Ds of Distraction, Duration and Distance. Each of these will create a higher level of difficulty for the dog. When proofing a behaviour, only work on one D at a time. If you lump together too many steps, the dog may not understand what you want or mean. If your dog has been able to complete a behaviour in one place but fails somewhere else, look at the Ds to see if you have missed valuable steps in their learning. Did you move from the garden to the park and want your Border Collie to hold his sit for longer? If so, you have increased the level of distraction *and* the duration. Maybe you were also a step further away from your dog, so you increased distance as well.

Some dogs need more steps than others when proofing their behaviour. For me, Mini and Ding were opposite ends of the spectrum. Ding could learn something in the house and take it to other environments straight away, whereas Mini lacked confidence in learning. She needed to learn things in the living room, then by the living room door, then with the door open before moving just outside the door. While she needed lots more steps, being taught this way gave her really solid behaviours. Having a dog like Ding, who is so quick to learn, can come back to bite you in the bum when all of a sudden you realise their understanding wasn't as good as you thought. It can also make you a lazy trainer or a poor trainer who expects this from all dogs.

Exercise Nine

I am often asked how long a dog should be trained each day. This exercise in your workbook will help you work out how to meet your dog's needs with physical exercise, mental training, emotional support and social needs. Each dog has their own personal recipe for the perfect day and this will help you work out what your dog needs to live their best life.

https://www.dingbattdogtraining.co.uk/workbook

Key Learning Points

- Advanced training is the basics done really well.
- You will recycle back to foundations throughout your training journey. This is normal and does not mean you are not making progress.
- You can't train away pain or a poor diet.
- Teaching a behaviour is the quick part of the training. Proofing the behaviour so your dog can do it anywhere takes time.

Chapter Ten
Finding the Off Switch for a Harmonious Household

It is unhealthy for your dog to be in a constant state of arousal and can be tiresome for you as well. Think back to Chapter One, where we discussed the environmental differences between the farm Border Collie and the urban Border Collie. The farm Collie who lives in a kennel or shed will have a much more peaceful time than an urban Collie who is exposed to people moving around their house, TVs, noisy kitchen equipment, hoovers, people passing their house and external noise for many more hours a day. It is important to build quiet time into their lives so they can detox their sensitive senses from all the stimuli and allow their systems to calm. Alongside training, simple things such as making sure their bed is not in a place of heavy footfall can help them rest, as will not giving free access to toys in the house but keeping them for special play times.

Genetics means these working dogs keep going for long periods of time; they are persistent. Many Border Collies come with a faulty off switch and need to be taught they can be calm and don't have to be on the go or controlling everything that moves all the time.

A Border Collie may struggle to switch off and settle for many reasons. The most obvious reason is a lack of exercise, but many that have adequate exercise still can't switch off at home. In urban environments, overstimulation (visual or auditory) can contribute to their inability to settle. Constant play can become a habit and they become adrenalin junkies. It can become a vicious cycle where movement creates more dopamine, which can lead to them wanting to move more if we don't teach them a different way. Not teaching them what you want them to do and how to manage their emotions can also be a cause.

Teaching mat work can be so beneficial and is a core exercise in foundation training. I highly recommend teaching this from day one with puppies and rescue dogs, as well as older dogs who have not yet learnt this skill. This is not just to teach your dog to stay on a boundary but to help create a positive emotional calm response. In the dog training world, we refer to this as a conditioned emotional response or a CER. This means that their mat or bed becomes associated with a calm and relaxed feeling. If you send them to their mat, they will be able to calm more quickly and become more flexible in their arousal levels.

Once you have taught the behaviour, you can proof the mat work to be used in many different situations, which is why it is a great foundational skill to teach. It underpins a lot of other training with movement sensitivity. You can teach your Border Collie that they can be relaxed in the presence of movement. They can understand that they don't have to control the busy world around them, and it helps them feel more comfortable in our busier environments.

Mat work can be used as good manners when you are eating meals or cooking, or when going to pubs or cafes. It can also be used to change emotional responses to items like the hoover or be a place for your dog to go when the doorbell rings. Its use is endless and is beneficial to both you and your dog.

When you teach mat work, you are working to change your dog's emotional response so it is important to protect the mat at all times from stressful situations. Therefore, if you used it in a café and a dog approached that your dog was not sure of, you would ask your dog to get up so they don't connect the mat with a stressful situation. Always keep the dog safe on the mat to protect the emotional response that you want to create.

Changing an emotional response can take time. We all know that if someone tells you to relax, it is harder, just like if someone tells you not to think about pink elephants, you immediately picture a pink elephant. But with patience, repetition and time, your dog will learn that their mat has a feel-good factor.

An example of this is my own dog, Ding. When he was younger, he could resource guard against my elderly spaniel. As soon as I saw him start to eye her, stiffen or lift his lip, I would cue him to move away to his mat. I used a light and cheery voice so it was not a punishment. Because we had already conditioned the mat to feel good, we could almost sense his relief as he trotted to his mat. Guarding is usually due to stress and in this example, Ding learnt to relieve his stress by making a better choice to go to his mat as an incompatible but alternative behaviour.

Mat work training is an important foundation skill for Border Collies to learn to cope with all the unnatural movement that they can find overstimulating in our busy urban environments and homes. Once you have taught mat work, you can introduce moving distractions in order to work through reactions to the TV, household items or the hoover by starting with really small movements.

A relaxed dog in the home will also find it easier to cope in the outside world. Stress in the home will mean that their baseline stress level is higher and they will be less able to cope with any further stress. The dog will trigger stack more quickly, and this could affect his behaviour on walks: he may be more reactive or not listen to cues such as his recall. Stress can also increase possible chase behaviours. The overall positive effect of teaching the Border Collie an off switch is therefore far-reaching.

Border Collie Academy member Victoria has worked so hard to help her dog Lenny fit into family life. Using mat work he is able to settle on a bed in the garden while they play tennis. He also makes a brilliant ball boy when asked to collect the balls, so he is included in the game. This is a great example of how to help a Border Collie thrive in a family's urban home. He can stay calm in the presence of movement while also being fully included in fun and games.

Exercise Ten

How to Teach Mat Work

To teach mat work, use a piece of vet bed, a towel, your dog's bed or anything that you can ask your dog to lie down on. While some keep a specific mat for this exercise that they can take wherever they go, I tend to generalise to different objects depending on what I point at. This helps if I ever forget to take their one specific mat with me.

1. To start with, to get your dog interested in the mat, drop some treats on it so it becomes a good place to be. If your dog knows a down cue, you can ask them into a down on the mat. If you are starting right at the beginning with a dog with no learning history, when they are on the mat, hold some treats under your hand and wait until they offer a down, then lift your hand and allow them the treats.
2. Once your dog understands the down, start to drop treats in an arc from in front of your dog until you are by their side. They should then pop over onto their hip into a settle position. We want to encourage a settle position rather than a sphinx down as the posture is more relaxing for the dog, and a relaxed body will help create a relaxed mind.
3. Teach a release cue so that your dog starts to understand that they should only get up when released. You can use a cue like 'OK', 'Break' or 'Free'. With your dog in the settle, say your release word and throw a treat off the mat so the dog gets up to get it.

4. Stay by the mat when you release the dog and the dog should orient back to the mat. Help them into a settle position again. When they start to return to the mat and put themselves into the settle position with less help from you, then teach the 'On Your Mat' cue by saying the cue once the dog has eaten the treat they were released to.
5. Build desire for the dog to want to get onto the mat by gently restraining your dog just off the mat by either a finger in their collar or a hand across their chest. Say your cue and release them and they should go onto the mat and into a settle position where you will reward them. Release them from the mat to a treat and then gradually add a little distance so the dog starts to understand to go to the mat from anywhere. Don't increase the distance too much each time. A step back each time is enough. If your dog struggles, you can start by taking a step with them towards the mat and then build to you standing still.
6. To start to build duration on the mat, you can create a delay between the rewards. Reward as soon as the dog lies down. At first, you may have to drop a treat every second, but then add small pauses between treats. Start with a two-second delay, then a three-second delay. When building the duration, don't always count to a higher number, as this drastically reduces the rate of reinforcement and makes it less worthwhile (from the dog's perspective) to stay on the mat. Instead, change from a continuous rate of reinforcement to a variable

rate of reinforcement. You might reward after two seconds, one second, three seconds, two seconds, five seconds, then one second and gradually increase the time between rewards.

7. Now it is time for you to move while your dog stays on the mat. Start with one step away and then back towards your dog to reward. For some dogs, you may even need to start by moving your feet on the spot while you reward. Again, gradually build the number of steps you can move away from your dog while they are on the mat. Use the same variable rate of reinforcement as before to increase the distance.

8. Now you can start to proof the training in ways you will use it in real life, so practise walking to the table and sitting down as if you were having your dinner. Can you turn your back on the dog, or make a cup of tea, or walk out of the room? Try to vary the distractions so your dog doesn't just think they have to stay still while you move around. Otherwise, when you want to sit down and be still, they may think it is time to get up.

9. Once taught at home, you need to generalise the training to different environments, such as a café or a bench on a walk. Dogs do not generalise their training in the same way we do, so when you take your mat to other environments, you will need to re-teach the skill *and* use a higher rate of reinforcement if the environment is more difficult until they understand the skill in many different contexts.

Key Learning Points

- Many Border Collies need to be taught to relax, as it doesn't come naturally.
- There is a difference between teaching your dog to stay and conditioning a calm emotional response.
- Mat work can be used to help your dog stay relaxed, as an alternative incompatible behaviour and also to change the Border Collie's emotions about movement.

Chapter Eleven
Impulse Control for Your Border Collie: Build a Stronger Bond

Teaching your Border Collie to be calm is not the solution to everything. Another foundation skill they should learn is impulse control. If your Border Collie is overexcited, expecting them to just be calm may be a step too far. Excitement is a natural emotional state; you can't expect them to be calm all the time. But when this excitement tips over too far, they can sometimes lose their ability to think and then cannot respond to you. You therefore also need to teach them to be able to think while in arousal.

Border Collies are bred to be impulsive so they can make quick decisions when controlling the flock. It is important to teach your pet Border Collie to have impulse control so they don't take it upon themselves to control everything that moves and so they are able to listen to you. A dog in control of their impulses will be able to listen more and stay safer than one who reacts to things without thinking first. A working Border Collie does need to be more independent in their thinking while working livestock, as it is too late to respond to a sheep if they need to look to the farmer or shepherd before taking action. Despite this, they should still be under control and not round up the flock without the shepherd's say so. A pet Border Collie has many more things in their environment that move, and without training they may take it upon themselves to try to control lots of things you don't want them to. Family members or visitors to the house, cars, cyclists, joggers or even other dogs can become prime targets.

An adolescent dog naturally becomes more impulsive due to their development. As a general guide, adolescence is between about six months and two years of age. Unsurprisingly, this is also the time when most dogs are rehomed due to a deterioration in their behaviour. So even if your puppy was angelic, had a great recall and seemed to have great social skills, they may have become more frustrated, reactive or more inclined to chase things they previously appeared to have no interest in. More management may be needed during this time so they can't practise unwanted behaviour while you add more value to the behaviour you do want. Management may mean using a long line to support the recall or temporarily taking them to less distracting environments while their hormones settle.

It is not uncommon for behaviours such as car chasing to start during this time, along with a reduction in their recall response.

Many people refer to their dog as stubborn, but I always encourage them to rethink this term. There are many reasons why your dog may not immediately do what you want. The dog may not understand what is being asked of them. They may lack confidence to offer the behaviour or they may have a conflict of motivators. They may not want to come in from the garden as they are enjoying being outside, and if they come inside, the fun stops. The cue to ask them to come in has not been taught to a level where it happens automatically even though the fun may stop when they come into the house.

In this scenario, your dog is making a choice to do their preferred activity. Choice is something you should also consider. Having choices can empower you and your dog. When a dog comes into your home, many of their choices are removed. They eat the food we give them, at the time we want to feed them. They go for a walk when and where we want to go. They don't get much choice in the way they live. In the dog training world, we are encouraged to give our dogs more choices to enrich their lives. However, we should only give them choices when we know they won't make a poor decision.

You can offer different types of food. You can offer a choice of toy to play with and work for. Let them choose the route of the walk as long as it is safe to do so. Give them the choice to opt out of handling through teaching voluntary handling – start and stop button behaviours can help build your dog's confidence. But you do not want your dog to inappropriately choose to chase a child or car because they lack control of their impulses on a walk.

The Premack principle is a well-known technique to shape your dog's behaviour. They offer you a lesser desired behaviour to get access to the thing they want. It is named after work undertaken in the 1960s by David Premack, a psychologist. An example of this principle is when a child is told to eat their vegetables so they can have a pudding or dessert. They have to offer the lesser desired behaviour of eating some vegetables to get what they want. In dog training, you may want your dog to look at you when they see something they want to 'ask permission' to access it. Your dog may love to swim and when they see water, if they look at you, they may be released to go for a swim. This principle works well as the dog gets the thing most rewarding to them and builds value in lesser desired behaviours, which in turn become more valuable to the dog as they become paired with good things. As the training becomes stronger, your dog will automatically start to check in with you when he sees things he would love to chase rather than just taking off to do them without giving you a second thought.

Teaching your dog impulse control will have a positive effect on many aspects of their life. It will help as part of recall training, so the dog will offer automatic check-ins. It will mean they are safer due to not running straight out of doorways or chasing after cars. The more control you have, the more freedom your dog can be allowed to run safely off-lead on walks when in appropriate off-lead areas.

There are times, for certain dogs, when I don't encourage the use of impulsivity training. This is usually if the dog is scared or has areas where they need to build confidence. Some dogs may appear impulsive in certain aspects of their life yet fearful in others. Look at what the dog is telling you. Do they need to learn to control their impulses in this type of situation or not? For example, if a dog is scared to leave the house, I wouldn't use impulse control at the doorway. I don't mean I would never teach any impulse control training with these dogs, but that it would be kept appropriate to just the situations where the dog could not control their impulses. I may not train doorway manners to a dog that is nervous about leaving the house, but if they were impulsive about grabbing food from your plate, I would teach them impulse control around taking food. I use a lot of play with fearful dogs to build their optimism. Once I have built their play drive, I add impulse control around the toy, but not until the dog is really keen on play, or it may lessen their play drive.

Below is an example of an impulse control exercise for use when exiting the house or vehicle. By teaching a dog not to go through doorways until released, they will be safer if a door is ever left open. It will prevent them from pushing through if visitors come to the house, and will set them up for successful walking rather than being like a whirlwind right from the **start. If** you struggle with your dog pulling on their lead, set them up for success by exiting the house under control first.

Exercise Eleven

Doorway Manners

Leaving the house in an orderly manner sets the tone for the whole walk. It also keeps the dog safe from running straight out of the door into oncoming traffic. Leaving the house in a thoughtful manner also helps them to be able to walk on a loose lead. They will be in a better headspace than if they are allowed to barge out of the door and then expected to control themselves in a more interesting or exciting environment.

If your dog struggles to learn this on the door you exit the house by, you can initially teach it on an internal door so there is less excitement and they should find it easier to learn.

1. Approach the door with your dog on a lead. Cue the dog to sit. Reward them for sitting. Now touch the door handle and then reward your dog for staying in a sit. If they get up at any time, just be patient and ask them to sit again. If you have to reset the sit, do not then reward the dog, or some smart dogs will get up so you can reset and reward them.
2. When you can touch the handle and the dog can stay in a sit, start to move the handle but without opening the door. Reward your dog for staying in the sit.
3. Now open the door an inch and close it again, and reward your dog.
4. Systematically build to be able to fully open the door. If the dog gets up just shut the door and wait for the dog to offer a sit again and restart.
5. Once you can open the door, take a step forward and reward your dog for staying in the sit. Build to being able to walk out of the door while your dog waits.
6. Use your release cue to release your dog from the sit and allow them through the door. Once through, cue them for a sit and reward the sit. Shut the door, then release your dog from the sit and enjoy your walk.

The sit on the outside of the door generally takes longer to achieve than the one on the inside due to the environment.

Your long-term aim with this exercise is to be able to remove the sit cues, and for the context of the door to be the cue for your dog to offer the sit. This is helpful because if the door is accidentally left open, the dog should understand not to go through it without being released, so it is a safety factor as well as a good exercise for impulse control.

If you struggle with the sit on the outside of the door, you can always take the dog back inside and start again. This helps break the pattern of them always expecting to proceed forward rather than wait.

When you think of what your dog finds most rewarding, you can also remove the treats from the equation once they understand the exercise, as going through the door is usually the most rewarding thing.

Key Learning Points

- Border Collies are bred to be impulsive; they need to be to respond quickly to livestock.
- Teaching your Border Collie impulse control will help keep them safe.
- In adolescence, they will naturally become more impulsive.
- The Premack principle means the dog has to offer a lesser desired behaviour to gain access to something they want.
- Teaching impulse control at doorways can help you start your walk with your dog in a better headspace and under more control.

Chapter Twelve
The Nervous Border Collie: How to Build Confidence and Trust

While this book has mainly discussed herding instincts and misplaced herding behaviour, there is another category of Border Collie. Some Border Collies are more sensitive. They have anxiety, noise sensitivity or are generally more fearful. Some do not even want to leave the house to go for a walk. There are, however, differences between dogs even within this category in that anxiety is a fear of something that hasn't happened yet, and so the stimulus is not present. Fear is of a stimulus that is present.

It is important to always rule out any health or pain issues with these dogs as there is a large correlation between poor health or pain and behavioural issues or fearful behaviour, especially generalised noise sensitivity.

There are many factors that may lead to a more nervous type of temperament. Genetics combined with the dog's environment will affect how confident the dog is (or isn't).

Genetics and epigenetics are important when selecting a pup. A stressed bitch passes on stress hormones to the pups. Bitches that show less nurturing traits also raise less secure pups. It has been shown in epigenetics that stress can create changes in the DNA that can be passed through to future generations.

This has been shown in mice which were exposed to the scent of cherry blossom (acetophenone) while also being exposed to an electric shock. Mice whose father or grandfather had learned to associate this smell with a shock and fear were shown to be more jumpy when presented with the same odour than normal mice, even when exposed to lower concentrations than the normal mice. This demonstrates that fear can be passed through generations and why we should consider genetics when selecting a pup.

While some dogs may be nervous from the start, others may become nervous later in life. If this is the case, we need to look for the cause of this change. I have worked with some Border Collies who did not want to leave the house, and it was thought they were scared of the outdoor environment. While this was true for some, for others, it was a dislike of having a harness put on that caused them to cower away from their owners. When the owner switched to using a flat collar and lead, the dog happily went for a walk.

One-time scary events can cause long-standing issues just as much as continuous exposure to stressful events. My own dog Mini became scared one New Year when my neighbour let off fireworks just behind my house without telling me. They were extremely loud and came down into my courtyard and onto the kitchen roof. Until that day, Mini had shown no signs of any noise sensitivity. The following night, she did not want to go out to the toilet after dark. We then had heavy rain and a thunderstorm. She generalised her stress to heavy rain because she was still stressed from the fireworks. I live in the countryside where there is a lot of shooting in the winter months. The gunshots followed as a third trigger. All this happened because of a one-time event which was out of my control.

Mini's scenario is an example of trigger stacking and how she generalised fear to more triggers, even ones she had previously been ok with. Trigger stacking is an accumulation of stresses which add up to push the dog over the threshold so they can no longer listen and respond. They may start the day at a low level of stress but meet many stimuli on their walk. They may be ok passing the first three dogs or cars, but when the fourth comes along, their window of tolerance has been exceeded, and they react. At this point, all the stress has added up and the dog is over the threshold. They react to smaller triggers they could otherwise have coped with. When the dog has become trigger-stacked and gone over threshold, they will need to increase the distance from their triggers to be able to calm enough to become responsive. The higher a dog's baseline stress level, the lower their tolerance to stress. They may also be unable to recover from stress as quickly as a more resilient dog and may only start to recover when they are back in a place of safety.

It is important to provide safety and security to encourage confidence and resilience in your dog and not to lose your dog's trust by putting them in situations they are uncomfortable with. Being aware of your dog's body language to identify when they feel pressured, anxious or fearful will help you support your dog.

While it is not your fault if you have a dog who is nervous, it is important to note that you can affect how your dog feels. If you already feel nervous yourself and you are with a friend who is acting jumpy and telling you how scared they are, you are likely to start to feel that way too. But if you are with someone who is calm and confident, you are likely to feel better. It is the same for your dog. If they are nervous and you hold them on a tight lead so they can't escape, it would be understandable if this made them more scared. We also give off pheromones that they can smell, and we change our breathing and heart rate, which they also pick up on. So being able to stay calm and confident within yourself helps your dog.

One study of horses and their handlers showed a link between handler anxiety and that of the horse. The handlers were told that a person was going to open an umbrella just as they passed. The person did not open the umbrella, but the heart rates of the handler and horse *both* raised just from the handler being told that something was going to happen. It seems reasonable to believe that a dog's feelings can be affected by their human's feelings, similarly to those of a horse.

The first step to lower stress levels in an anxious dog should be to lower the baseline stress in their home environment. Look for causes of stress within the home. Is the dog being intimidated by another dog in the household, and therefore constantly living on their nerves and unable to fully relax? Remove pressure from the dog, provide a safe place for them, and advocate for them. Work on improving their sleep routine and provide a healthy diet. Giving time away from lots of visual movement and noise can be especially beneficial to a Border Collie as a sensory detox. Also look to increase enrichment and positive experiences in your dog's life.

Panksepp discovered seven emotional systems in neuroscience. Only one of these systems can operate at any one time. They cannot operate concurrently. They are Fear, Play, Seeking, Care, Rage, Lust, Panic/Grief. If your dog is playing or seeking, they can't be fearful as well. This is why two of my favourite ways to help a sensitive or less confident dog are play and scent work. The fear pathway is slightly stronger, though, so you need to build their desire to play and seek before you can use them in gradually more difficult environments through counter conditioning and desensitisation. It is worth spending time building your dog's desire to play and seek at a time when they feel safe, rather than using the games when noise or scary situations happen. Otherwise, you can inadvertently pair play with the scary thing and poison the game rather than increase its value.

Working on a dog's body awareness and proprioception can help them feel more grounded and balanced in their body. Exposing them carefully to new experiences, new surfaces and teaching them body awareness through canine fitness or movement puzzles can help them feel more confident.

Nervous dogs may react in different ways. They may shut down and freeze in learned helplessness, which should not be confused with a dog being quiet and well-behaved. They may panic and want to run away. Some resort to misplaced or inappropriate herding behaviour to make themselves feel better, because herding and controlling are intrinsically rewarding. Because they are nervous, though, it can lead to nipping rather than just being quietly in control.

I am often asked what to do when a dog refuses to move on a walk or panics and tries to run away. How I respond depends on the situation and the individual dog. If the dog is spooked by something they can see that is an inanimate object, I may just wait for the dog and give them time to look and work it out, as I know they aren't in danger. They may then inch forward to investigate in their own time. I would not lure them with food towards the object they are scared of, as this may lose the dog's trust, but I may approach the object myself and calmly stand by it to show the dog it isn't going to move or hurt them. If the stimulus is moving, I may walk the dog in an arc to maintain a distance they feel comfortable enough to stay below threshold. Don't make your dog stay still on a tight lead and make them feel they have no escape route.

If the stimulus is not something that can be seen, I will judge the dog to see if I think I can help them through it with a jolly *'let's go'* or if I need to abort the walk and take them back to the car or house to recover.

All sentient beings need agency. They need to be able to make choices for themselves and not be pressured into situations they don't want to be in. There is, however, a fine line here in helping build your dog's resilience. Border Collies love clarity and rules, and this can alleviate stress, but giving agency where it is safe to do so is also empowering. They shouldn't be given choices where they can make a poor choice and fail or be put in a situation they wouldn't want to be in, but allowing them to choose the route you walk or the toys they play with empowers them.

You can use agency in their training to remove pressure from the dog and avoid situations of flooding where they become overwhelmed and or shut down due to being in too stressful an environment. Teaching start button behaviours for handling can be empowering and build confidence. Teaching your dog to learn through shaping, but rewarding them equally whether they engage or disengage, can remove the pressure of learning.

Alongside choice and control come patterns and predictability. Control Unleashed is a system of dog training developed by Leslie McDevitt and heavily based on pattern games. Using patterns brings predictability to the dog so they know what is coming next and feel safer. They also don't need to use as much brain energy to work things out. As well as helping dogs function in different environments, the exercises (such as Look at That) help to counter condition triggers the dog may have.

Helping dogs decompress can speed up their recovery from certain events as well as lower overall baseline stress. Massage, teaching the dog to Take a Breath, stretching exercises and encouraging naturally self-calming behaviours such as licking, sniffing or chewing are all beneficial.

For dogs that are noise sensitive, some ideas to help are ear defenders or snoods to help block out the noise. Body wraps or thunder shirts can give a feeling of comfort. These should all be worn and got used to before the sounds start so they are not just associated with the scary noises. Playing music such as Taiko drums, jazz or classical music can also help.

I have bought ear defenders for Mini and some puzzle games that she will interact with when there is a thunderstorm. She also likes to be close to me for comfort. Ding loves to play games with balls or toys. My other two dogs are happy and relaxed and don't worry, although Beau did have some experiences when young that really scared him. We were outside when a low, screeching jet flew over us. He screamed and bolted for the house.

For two weeks he was worried about anything in the sky and even looked worriedly at the ceiling if he heard a sound outside the house. At first, when I saw him behaving like this I ignored him and carried on with what I was doing to show there was nothing to be scared of. Once he had built up some resilience again, I then actively started to work on noise exercises with him. I shaped him to knock over objects, progressing the noise they made. This way, he was in control of making the noises.

He already had good play drive, and so I used lots of play to build his optimism before adding noises while we were playing. To start with, I played at the same time as the noise and gradually built to the sound occurring, followed immediately with play. Beau has since competed in an agility competition where there was a clay pigeon shoot going on just the other side of the hedge and showed no worry at all.

Some say you shouldn't comfort your dog when they are scared, or you will reinforce their fear. I would argue that you can't reinforce an emotion, only a behaviour, and therefore it is ok to comfort your dog if they are scared of something. Emotions and behaviour are closely linked, however, so there is more nuance to it than that. If my dog wants to be comforted, I will comfort them but I don't overreact or panic if my dog spooks at something for the first time.

Another thing I like to do with dogs that lack confidence is to teach them to be cheeky. Teaching them to pickpocket and steal things from your pocket can be fun for both you and them. Encourage them to get excited and bark or to jump up and down on the spot. These are behaviours we usually want to stop our dogs from doing but they can actually be confidence building for a timid or nervous dog.

For some dogs who suffer generalised anxiety which affects their quality of life or ability to learn, working with a behaviourist and vet who can prescribe behavioural medications can help as part of a behaviour modification programme. They should not be used alone to try to 'fix' a problem, but they may help the dog be able to learn alongside a training programme. These medications should not sedate the dog and can help improve the quality of life of some dogs.

Exercise Twelve

Teach your dog through shaping to become more confident around noises by interacting with items that make a noise. Teaching the shaping concept helps to build confidence in working out solutions rather than immediately reacting. This exercise also gives the dog control over making the noise. For examples of this exercise check out your workbook.

https://www.dingbattdogtraining.co.uk/workbook

Key Learning Points

- Rule out pain or health issues as a root cause of anxiety or fear.
- Both genetics and the environment will affect your dog's natural confidence level.
- One-time scary events or continuous exposure to stressful events can cause longer-standing issues for the dog.
- The first step to helping a nervous dog should be to lower baseline stress levels.
- Play, giving the dog agency, patterns and scent work can all help build a dog's confidence.

Chapter Thirteen
Working With Your Border Collie

I hope this book has helped you understand your Border Collie on a deeper level and that you have been able to implement some of the exercises to work towards your training goals.

If you haven't already downloaded the workbook, you can do so here to help you apply your learning to your own Border Collie, since every individual dog is different. Applying the knowledge in a practical way is how true learning takes place.

https://www.dingbattdogtraining.co.uk/workbook

This book began by looking at what Border Collies were bred for. Even though you may keep your dog as a pet, they are still a working breed dog. Throughout this book, you have been encouraged to recognise the Border Collie working traits within your own dog and to identify misplaced or inappropriate herding type behaviour. You will have learned why many Border Collies struggle in urban environments and that they need mental training as well as physical exercise to prevent them going self-employed.

You now understand how the Border Collie breed is often misunderstood and that you need to look at your dog through a breed-specific lens. The exercise at the end of Chapter Two helped you recognise and understand what drives your dog's behaviour, which then guided you in choosing the appropriate training techniques.

Chapter Three helped you identify how unique your Border Collie really is. Not only are they incredibly intelligent, learning equally quickly both wanted and unwanted behaviours, they are also unique in their makeup. Their movement sensitive eyes are structured differently from those of many other breeds, which can be problematic if misunderstood. Eyeing behaviour is intrinsically rewarding to the Border Collie, and unless we teach them how to focus on us and control these impulses, they can herd inappropriately and want to control cars, cyclists and joggers.

Border Collies work with different styles. A nervous Border Collie with a strong eye can lie down and refuse to move as they are in conflict between staring and not feeling brave enough to control the oncoming moving trigger. If you have a dog that does this, they are likely a clapper. Their uniqueness isn't confined to their eyes as they also have more dopamine in their basal ganglia than most other breeds, which creates a desire to move and to keep going in their work. This can become a vicious cycle if you don't teach them an off switch.

Learning about body language in Chapter Four helped you read your dog on a deeper level and aid in your communication with them. Being able to recognise when your Border Collie switches from calmly observing the environment to when they fixate their stare and want to control with their eyes is hugely important in their training. By cueing the dog to do an alternative behaviour before they go over threshold and therefore can't respond to you any more is essential for successful training. The practical exercise helped you take an in-depth look at your own dog and practise observing their body language in different situations so you can prevent them needing to escalate behaviour to make their thoughts and feelings clearer.

In Chapter Five, you learned how to avoid common training mistakes and how to set your dog up for success. While it is always easier to prevent a behaviour occurring than to change it once it has developed, thinking of how to help your Border Collie succeed is an essential part of any training plan. This is especially important if you keep your Border Collie in an urban environment. Not all Border Collies need to live on farms and work livestock to lead a fulfilling life, but being able to recognise the difference between over-stimulation and over-exercise, you will avoid some of the most common unwanted behavioural issues from occurring.

It is not always possible to prevent all unwanted behaviour. Living with a dog that has challenging behaviour can impact your own mindset. Be kind to yourself and know you are doing the best you can with the information you have, just like your dog. Remember that emotions only last for around ninety seconds; after this time, it is the stories we build around events that can lead us into a negative spiral. Don't let a whole walk be ruined by just one negative experience. Try to reframe any challenges as opportunities to train. Training is an ongoing journey, not an event. Be sure to make the training journey fun for both yourself and your dog.

While some Border Collies are more challenging than dogs from many other breeds, it is often the dogs we have to work harder with that we develop the deepest bonds and relationships with. Having to learn to read them and work with them builds deeper understanding and connection. If you are struggling at the moment, know that with the right help you can improve your dog's behaviour.

Border Collies are highly intelligent and they learn all the time. If we don't work with them, they will still learn from the environment they are in. If we allow the environment to become more rewarding than ourselves, then our recall is more likely to fail. Teaching focus and attention is an important skill for our Border Collies, who find staring at things intrinsically rewarding.

As part of the training process, it is important to understand how dogs don't generalise as well as we do. While some Border Collies learn incredibly quickly and can translate those skills to different environments, dogs generally are much more contextual in their learning so need to be retaught behaviours in many different environments for the cues to be thoroughly understood.

Advanced training is the basics done really well. Don't be afraid to spend time on the foundation skills; build value in your rewards and the value will transfer into your training. It is never a backwards step to revisit the foundation skills. In fact, this should be encouraged. Keep your foundations strong throughout your dog's life and you won't go far wrong.

Teaching your Border Collie to switch off and settle will help you create a calm household. This foundation skill can be used for a multitude of things, such as calm behaviour when the doorbell rings or around your meal times. For Border Collies, it is especially useful for helping them stay calm in the presence of moving things that could otherwise be triggers for inappropriate herding behaviour.

Alongside teaching an off switch, impulse control is another foundation skill to work on with our naturally impulsive genius Border Collies. Impulse control training will help them learn to check in with you to ask permission for access to things they want, improve your recall, and keep them safe.

While the majority of Border Collies can benefit from impulse control training, if they are nervous it is more important to build their confidence first. Play skills are important for all types to build confidence and your relationship. Play can help build optimism in the more nervous dog and can be a useful training tool when working with noise sensitivity. As with all training, make sure that it is enjoyable and fun for both handler and dog. Fun is intrinsically rewarding and gives a feel-good factor.

Here again is the link to download the workbook to accompany this book. I suggest revisiting the exercises once a month to check your progress and add to the exercises with your newfound knowledge.

https://www.dingbattdogtraining.co.uk/workbook

I appreciate that not everything can be learned from a book. Nor can a book give you feedback on your training. However, you can take the next step and gain further support when you seek me out in my online membership The Border Collie Academy.

Within this breed-specific membership, I include even more knowledge and information. Most valuably of all, you can also gain feedback on your training videos seven days a week so you know the exact next steps for you and your dog to keep progressing on the right track. You can also learn from video feedback offered to other members who are working through the same training challenges within our friendly and supportive community.

The Border Collie Academy is like a library full of Border Collie knowledge. You won't need to read every book in the library to get the answers you need, as there is something for everyone. Here are just some of the modules:

Foundation Modules
- Teach Your Collie to Be Calm - so you can fix that faulty off switch and have a harmonious household
- Impulse Control - to create a dog who listens to you
- Loose Lead Legends - so your walks are more enjoyable and your arm isn't pulled out of its socket
- Recall for DingBatts - so your dog comes back each and every time

Training in the Real World Modules
- DingBatts Unleashed - for a more focused dog
- Playing with DingBatts - to build play as a valuable reward and improve your relationship
- Proofing Behaviours - so your training works in all environments, no matter how distracting
- Collie Confidence - to build your dog's resilience

- Give Me That! - teach your dog to bring you items and how to avoid resource guarding

Skills and Fun Modules

- Scentsational Scentwork - teach your dog to use their nose and their brain
- Upskills - to uplevel your training skills so you can communicate clearly with your dog
- Advent Calendars - with fun activities, tricks to teach your dog and recipes

Collie Behaviour Modules

- Car Chasing to Calm - for safer, stress-free walks
- Bark Busters - for a calmer household
- The Movement Sensitive Collie - to teach your Border Collie they don't have to herd everything that moves
- Reactivity - to make your walks more enjoyable
- Enrichment - to give your Border Collie their best life
- Trick and Treat module - to help your dog's noise sensitivity and improve their resilience

There are also modules for voluntary handling protocols to take the stress out of vet visits and grooming, as well as opportunities to work towards your DingBatt Certificates and Trick Titles.

To see a full list of all that is included within the Border Collie Academy use the following link.

https://courses.dingbattdogtraining.co.uk/academy-bcb

Or check out our other courses on the website:
www.dingbattdogtraining.co.uk

It is time to go out and live your best life with your Border Collie, whether that be at competitions, changing his behaviour or teaching new fun tricks. Most of all, enjoy and appreciate your dogs every day: they are not with us for long enough.

If you have enjoyed this book, please share a photo of you and your dog with the book on social media and be sure to tag me.

@Sarahhedderly-Dingbattdogtraining
https://www.facebook.com/sarahhedderlydingbattdogtraining/

@DingBatt_Dog_Training
https://www.instagram.com/DingBatt_Dog_Training

@dingbattdogtraining
https://www.tiktok.com/@dingbattdogtraining

@dingbattdogtraining8673
https://www.youtube.com/@dingbattdogtraining8673

About the Author

Sarah lives in Somerset in the UK. Her first memories of Border Collies are of those which belonged to her grandad, who had a working farm. Little did she know that Scotty and Mick, the black tri Border Collies, would have such a long-lasting effect on her life. Scot was the older of the two and had a sleek, shiny coat. Mickey, the younger, had a curly coat and a huge character. He used to wrap his paws around Sarah to stop her from leaving him.

Sarah wasn't allowed her own dog at home when she was younger as her Dad was scared of dogs after being bitten as a child. But at sixteen years old, she got a lift to a local farm and came home with her first dog, a black tri Border Collie puppy whom she named Kim. Kim was what Sarah now refers to as a unicorn Collie. She was an easy dog who went out riding with her, learnt tricks and later accompanied Sarah to show jumping shows with her horses.

Kim was joined by Pip, another Border Collie, and then a Jack Russell called Smartie. After losing Kim, Sarah didn't feel able to have another Border Collie as she didn't want to compare them to Kim, and so along came Spring, the Springer Spaniel, and then Mini, the Mini American Shepherd, before Sarah decided it was time to return to Border Collies.

She adopted DingBatt, a five-month-old Border Collie puppy from Battersea Dogs Home and he has now been joined by Beau and Sparkles too.

Sarah worked as a McTimoney Animal Therapist for over twenty years, but it was Mini who was the first dog that encouraged Sarah to learn to be a trainer. Mini was a sensitive dog, and Sarah learnt to break down her training into lots of steps to support Mini in her learning. Ding was the complete opposite, a child genius who had been allowed to develop lots of unwanted behaviours. He learned both wanted and unwanted behaviour equally quickly, and he wasn't afraid of using his teeth to get what he wanted!

It was due to Ding that Sarah decided to specialise in working with Border Collies. Prior to Covid, she ran classes working mostly with reactivity through the Control Unleashed system of dog training. She was the first person in the UK to be awarded the CCUI, which is the Certified

About the Author

Control Unleashed Instructor qualification. When Covid hit, she started teaching online and specialised in Border Collies by setting up the Border Collie Academy, her online membership. Since then, she has worked with thousands of Border Collies from all around the globe, helping their owners transform their DingBatt Border Collies into Dreamboats.

Border Collies are Sarah's passion. She regularly sees the struggles people have when they expect the unicorn Collie but instead end up with a more challenging dog. Unfortunately, rescue centres are now overflowing and Border Collies, being a working breed, do not do well in this environment. Sarah's aim, therefore, is to educate people about the breed so they know what they are getting into. She wants to help people create the best relationship with their Border Collie so these amazing dogs can lead the lives they deserve.

Connect With the Author

Have you enjoyed this book? Would you like to stay in touch with me and keep learning about Border Collies? Fabulous!

You can follow me on social media:

f @Sarahhedderly-Dingbattdogtraining
https://www.facebook.com/sarahhedderlydingbattdogtraining/

◉ @DingBatt_Dog_Training
https://www.instagram.com/DingBatt_Dog_Training

♪ @dingbattdogtraining
https://www.tiktok.com/@dingbattdogtraining

▶ @dingbattdogtraining8673
https://www.youtube.com/@dingbattdogtraining8673

View my website: www.dingbattdogtraining.co.uk

And if you would like to join my private FB community where I host regular free training, you would be most welcome. Here is the link to join.

www.facebook.com/DingBattBorderCollieTraining

I have lots of free resources to share with you too, which might just help you and your Border Collie.

Grab them here: **www.dingbattdogtraining.co.uk/resources**

www.ingramcontent.com/pod-product-compliance
Lightning Source LLC
Chambersburg PA
CBHW060104230426
43661CB00033B/1411/J